Good Housekeeping Cookery Club

FRENCH

Maxine Clarke

EBURY PRESS
LONDON

First published 1996

1 3 5 7 9 10 8 6 4 2

First published in the United Kingdom in 1996 by Ebury Press, Random House, 20 Vauxhall Bridge Road, London SW1V 2SA

Random House Australia (Pty) Limited
20 Alfred Street, Milsons Point, Sydney,
New South Wales 2061, Australia

Random House New Zealand Limited
18 Poland Road, Glenfield,
Auckland 10, New Zealand

Random House South Africa (Pty) Limited
PO Box 337, Bergvlei, South Africa

Random House UK Limited Reg. No. 954009

A CIP catalogue record for this book is available from the British Library.

Managing Editor: JANET ILLSLEY
Design: SARA KIDD
Special Photography: LAURIE EVANS
Food Stylist: MAXINE CLARK
Assistant Food Stylist: SHEILA BRAIDWOOD
Photographic Stylist: LESLEY RICHARDSON
Techniques Photography: KARL ADAMSON
Food Techniques Stylist: ANGELA KINGSBURY
Recipe Testing: EMMA-LEE GOW

ISBN 0 09 180 959 2

Typeset in Gill Sans
Colour Separations by Digital Imaging (UK) Limited
Printed and bound in Italy by New Interlitho Italia S.p.a., Milan

CONTENTS

COOKERY NOTES

- Both metric and imperial measures are given for the recipes. Follow either metric or imperial throughout as they are not interchangeable.
- All spoon measures are level unless otherwise stated. Sets of measuring spoons are available in metric and imperial for accurate measurement of small quantities.
- Ovens should be preheated to the specified temperature. Grills should also be preheated. The cooking times given in the recipes assume that this has been done.

- Where a stage is specified in brackets under freezing, the dish should be frozen at the end of that stage.
- Size 2 eggs should be used except where otherwise specified. Free-range eggs are recommended.
- Use freshly ground black pepper and sea salt unless otherwise specified.
- Use fresh rather than dried herbs unless dried herbs are suggested in the recipe.
- Stocks should be freshly made if possible. Alternatively buy ready-made stocks or use good quality stock cubes.

INTRODUCTION

France was my first taste of a "foreign" country, as it is for so many of us. As a young Scottish teenager my initial visit in the late 60's was a revelation. The French attitude towards food was notably different from that of the British, which might be described as a rather puritanical denial of food as enjoyment. France may be close in proximity to Britain, but it is so very different culturally and gastronomically.

From an early age, French children are encouraged to appreciate food and its importance to family life. Meals bring everyone together to eat and talk ... and share the joys and cares of life. My love affair with France started from that holiday and is kept alive by frequent visits to our family house in quiet, rural Gascony.

France is an agricultural country with a multitude of climates and soils, and consequently produces most of her own fruit, vegetables, meat and poultry. There is still a tradition of weekly – sometimes even daily – markets which naturally become part of the way of life. To some extent this is changing with the onslaught of huge supermarkets on the outskirts of towns, but I'm sure the markets will always remain for the exchange of gossip, meeting of old friends and stocking up the larder. All of this produce is still eaten and appreciated seasonally, and home preserving for the winter months is still much a part of the way of life – even in towns.

The French have an eye for a bargain and shop astutely in the markets, carefully choosing the best product for the best price. This invariably involves long discussions with stall-holders in between. French people are not afraid to complain about inferior quality when shopping, or eating out. The recipient of the criticism will generally take it on board, discuss the problem animatedly or shrug it off in a gallic manner, but will not become hurt and offended, or treat you as if you had committed treason!

Although with modern transport regional foodstuffs can be bought outside their particular areas, the French still like to prepare local dishes at home and eat regional dishes in restaurants. Cooking in moderate restaurants is simple, using the best, fresh local ingredients. Be suspicious of long menus that promise all sorts of delights – these may include frozen or pre-prepared dishes. Fixed price menus generally offer great value, occasionally including wine in the price.

France has an extensive coastline spanning the North Sea, the Atlantic and the Mediterranean, and so has a wealth of fish and shellfish to enjoy. Even inland, larger towns boast a superb fish shop selling top quality fresh fish rushed from the coast that very morning.

Oysters are harvested in profusion and eaten with relish all over France, especially over the Christmas season – they are inexpensive and come in numerous sizes. Chunky fish soups are common on all coasts, Cotriade being one most suited to the type of fish available in Britain. Moules Frites are enjoyed in the North East of France, whereas Squid with Raito from Provence conjures up a taste of the past spice trade.

There is a rich diversity of traditional country dishes and, here, I have tried to give a broad selection from all areas of France. Bring a hint of the hot Mediterranean to the table with the basil and garlic-scented Soupe au Pistou. Sample a taste of Alsace with a creamy Leek Flan, release the scent of mountain herbs when you remove the lid of the Daube de Boeuf Niçoise, and discover the essence of Normandy with the delightful and refreshing Green Apple and Calvados Sorbet.

These recipes are not for the faint-hearted ... they are rich and flavourful, stemming from a country cuisine developed to satisfy ravenous appetites using farm produce and local ingredients, simply but lovingly prepared and cooked. Some may detect a South West bias – well they'd be right – my heart lies there! Bon Appetit!

MENU SUGGESTIONS

SPRING MENU

Starter
Asparagus with Poached Eggs
and Tarragon Cream

Main Course
Breton-style Lamb

Dessert
Green Apple Sorbet with Madeleines

SUMMER MENU

Starter
Salad of Bayonne Ham, Melon and Artichokes

Main Course
Seared Squid with Raito

Dessert
Pêches Cardinal
or
Tarte au Fromage Frais with Figs

AUTUMN MENU

Starter
Tourin

Main Course
Grilled Duck Breast with Maize 'Chips'

Dessert
Pear Tarte Renversée
or
Golden Custard Tart
with Plum Compote

WINTER MENU

Starter
Chicken and Duck Liver Terrine

Main Course
Daube de Boeuf Niçoise

Dessert
Walnut Cake with Crème Anglaise
or
Chocolate Crème Brulée

FISH MENU

Starter
Mouclade

Main Course
Seared Cod with Wilted Spinach and Beurre Blanc

Dessert
Tartelettes au Citron

GUIDE TO SAUCE-MAKING

These classic French sauces rely on the reduction of liquids to give an intense flavour, and the addition of either butter or eggs to enrich and thicken the sauce. They are relatively quick to make, but will not keep warm for long and are therefore best prepared just before serving.

BEURRE BLANC

A simple white wine sauce, delicious served with fish and white meats.
(Makes about 300 ml/½ pint)

225 g (8 oz) butter, chilled
2 shallots
45 ml (3 tbsp) white wine vinegar
45 ml (3 tbsp) white wine

1. Cut the butter into small cubes. Peel and finely chop the shallots. Put the vinegar, white wine and shallots in a very small saucepan. Bring to the boil and reduce to 15 ml (1 tbsp).

2. Over a low heat, gradually whisk in the butter, piece by piece, until the sauce begins to thicken as the butter starts to melt. Take the pan off and on the heat to prevent it overheating.

Note: If the sauce turns greasy and splits it has become too hot. If this happens, whisk in an ice-cube.

VARIATIONS

• Add 30 ml (2 tbsp) chopped fresh herbs to the finished sauce.
• For a red wine sauce, use red wine instead of the vinegar.
• For a rich mustard sauce, add 5 ml (1 tsp) drained green peppercorns in brine and 5 ml (1 tsp) Dijon mustard.

HOLLANDAISE

A wonderfully rich sauce to serve with hot or cold vegetables, such as steamed fresh asparagus and globe artichokes.
(Makes about 150 ml/¼ pint)

60 ml (4 tbsp) white wine vinegar
6 black peppercorns
1 mace blade
1 slice onion
1 bay leaf
3 egg yolks
150 g (5 oz) unsalted butter, at room temperature
30 ml (2 tbsp) single cream
lemon juice, to taste
salt and pepper

1. Put the vinegar in a small saucepan with the peppercorns, mace, onion slice and bay leaf. Bring to the boil and reduce to 15 ml (1 tbsp) liquid. Dip the base of the pan in cold water to stop further evaporation. Set aside.

2. Beat the egg yolks in a heatproof bowl with 15 g (½ oz) butter and a pinch of salt. Strain in the reduced vinegar. Place the bowl over a pan of barely simmering water and stir until beginning to thicken.

3. Beat in the remaining butter a piece at a time, until the mixture begins to thicken and emulsify. Ensure each addition of butter is incorporated before adding the next. Do not allow to overheat or the eggs will scramble and split.

4. Remove from heat, whisk in the cream, season and add lemon juice to taste. Serve at once.

SAVOURY SABAYON

This light, foamy emulsion is delicious with white fish, such as turbot or sole, and mixed seafood dishes. (Makes about 300 ml/½ pint)

300 ml (½ pint) fish or vegetable stock
3 egg yolks
175-225 g (6-8 oz) chilled unsalted butter, diced
salt and pepper

1. Pour the stock into a small saucepan, bring to the boil and reduce to 75 ml (5 tbsp) liquid. Dip the base of the pan in cold water to stop evaporation. Set aside to cool. Meanwhile, beat the egg yolks in a heatproof bowl with the reduced stock. Place the bowl over a pan of barely simmering water. Whisk over the heat for about 10 minutes until thick and foamy.

2. Whisk in the diced butter, a few pieces at a time, until the mixture begins to thicken and emulsify. Allow each addition of butter to be incorporated before adding the next; do not allow the mixture to overheat or the eggs will scramble and split. The sauce should be a thick pale lemon foam. Season with salt and pepper to taste. Serve immediately.

SWEET SABAYON

A delightful alternative to crème anglaise (page 74) or cream, to serve hot or cold with soft berries and all fruits. (Makes about 600 ml/1 pint)

200 g (7 oz) caster sugar
6 egg yolks
finely grated rind of 1 lemon
300 ml (½ pint) sweet dessert wine, such as Sauternes, or Muscat de Beaumes de Venise
150 ml (¼ pint) double cream, lightly whipped (optional)

Put the sugar, egg yolks and lemon rind into a large heatproof bowl (copper if available). Whisk over a pan of barely simmering water for about 10 minutes until the mixture is thick, pale and creamy. Slowly add the wine, whisking all the time, for about 5 minutes until the mixture is frothy, mousse-like and about twice the volume. Continue whisking for about 10 minutes until light but with dense bubbles. Serve immediately, or if serving cold, set the bowl over iced water and continue whisking for about 10 minutes or until completely cold, then fold in the cream.

GUIDE TO PASTRY-MAKING

You will find the quick methods for these essential French pastries within the appropriate recipes. If you have more time and a little patience it is well worth making these pastries by the traditional methods and freezing them in suitable quantities for later use. They will also keep in the refrigerator for up to 3 days. Both of these pastries are very different from the crumbly melt-in-the-mouth British shortcrust. They are more robust and tend not to crumble when baked – acting as strong containers for the filling.

PATE BRISEE

Literally meaning "broken dough", pâte brisée is a smooth malleable dough which is rolled out thinly. It is used for savoury tarts.

125 g (4 oz) plain white flour
50 g (2 oz) unsalted butter, at room
    temperature, cubed
1 egg yolk
pinch of salt

1. Sift the flour onto a clean work surface and make a large well in the centre.

2. Place the butter in the well with the egg yolk, salt and 22 ml (1½ tbsp) cold water.

3. Using the fingertips and a "pecking" motion, "peck" the butter, egg yolk, salt and water together until the mixture resembles scrambled eggs.

4. Gradually work in the flour, using the fingertips until the dough forms large crumbs. Add a little extra cold water if the dough looks too dry.

5. Lightly push the dough away from you, using the heel of your hand. Scrape together with a dough scraper or palette knife. Repeat until the dough is very smooth and pliable. Knead lightly to form a ball. Wrap tightly in cling film and chill for at least 30 minutes to relax the pastry and prevent shrinkage. Return to room temperature before rolling out.

PATE SUCREE

Pâte sucrée or pâte sablée becomes hard and biscuity when cooked. It is used mainly for fruit tarts. The high sugar content will make the pastry edges brown quickly – if necessary cover with a foil rim during baking.

125 g (4 oz) plain white flour
1.25 ml (¼ tsp) salt
50 g (2 oz) caster sugar
2 egg yolks
2.5 ml (½ tsp) vanilla essence
50 g (2 oz) butter, at room
　　temperature, cubed

1. Sift the flour onto a clean work surface and make a large well in the centre.

2. Place the salt, sugar, egg yolks and vanilla essence in the well and mix well with the fingertips of one hand to dissolve the sugar.

3. Add the cubed softened butter and using the fingertips, "peck" the sugar and egg mixture into the butter until the mixture resembles scrambled eggs.

4. Gradually work in the flour, using the fingertips until the dough forms large crumbs. If the dough looks too dry, add a little extra cold water.

5. Work the dough as for pâte brisée, pushing it with the heel of your hand against the work surface

and scraping it together with a palette knife until the dough is smooth and putty-like.

6. Gather up the dough and lightly knead together to form a ball. Wrap tightly in cling film and chill for at least 30 minutes to relax the pastry and prevent shrinkage. Let the pastry come to room temperature before rolling out to make it much easier to handle.

PASTRY QUANTITIES

These apply to both pâte brisée and pâte sucrée:
• A 125 g (4 oz) flour quantity will line an 18 cm (7 inch) flan tin
• A 175 g (6 oz) flour quantity will line a 23 cm (9 inch) flan tin
• A 225 g (8 oz) flour quantity will line a 28 cm (11 inch) flan tin

BRETON FISH SOUP

This chunky fish soup is made with two types of fish in Brittany — rich fish, like mackerel and sardines, and a selection of local white fish, similar to our cod and haddock. Enriched with fresh mussels, leeks, potatoes and sorrel, it rather resembles an American chowder. Its Breton name *cotriade* stems from the French word *côte*, meaning coast.

SERVES 6

450 g (1 lb) mussels in shells

450 g (1 lb) mixed mackerel,
    filleted sardines (optional)
    and monkfish, cleaned

450 g (1 lb) mixed white fish,
    such as cod, haddock,
    hake, whiting, cleaned

1 large onion, peeled

2 large leeks, trimmed

2 garlic cloves, peeled

50 g (2 oz) butter

450 g (1 lb) small old
    potatoes

900 ml (1½ pints) fish or
    vegetable stock

bouquet garni

salt and pepper

300 ml (½ pint) crème
    fraîche or double cream

350 g (12 oz) sorrel or
    spinach

TO SERVE

6 thick slices bread, toasted

6 garlic cloves, peeled

PREPARATION TIME
30 minutes, plus soaking
COOKING TIME
35 minutes
FREEZING
Not suitable

615 CALS PER SERVING

1. Scrub the mussels thoroughly and rinse well under cold running water. Pull away any 'beards', then place the mussels in a large bowl, cover with cold water and leave to soak for at least 30 minutes. Discard any opened ones that do not close when tapped sharply with the back of a knife.

2. If filleted, skin the fish and cut into large chunks. If whole, cut off the heads and slice into steaks. Pat dry on kitchen paper.

3. Slice the onion and leeks; chop the garlic. Melt the butter in a large flame-proof casserole or cooking pot. Add the onion, leeks and garlic and cook gently for about 5 minutes until soft but not coloured. Meanwhile, peel and quarter the potatoes. Add to the casserole and cook for 5 minutes, stirring occasionally. Add the stock, bouquet garni and seasoning. Bring to the boil, cover and simmer for about 10 minutes until the potatoes are almost tender.

4. Add the monkfish, mackerel and sardines; cook for 3 minutes. Add the remaining white fish and simmer for 5 minutes, then pour in the cream.

5. Finely shred the sorrel or spinach and carefully stir into the soup. Place the mussels on top and cover tightly.

Cook for 3 minutes or until the mussels have steamed open.

6. Serve immediately, from the pot, with a basket of toasted bread and a small bowl of garlic cloves. Each diner rubs a halved garlic clove over a slice of toast, places this on the bottom of a soup plate and ladles the soup on top.

NOTE: The potatoes should start to disintegrate and thicken the soup. If the soup looks too thick, add a little more stock.

TECHNIQUE

After soaking, tap the opened mussels sharply with the back of a knife. Any that do not close straight away are dead and must be discarded.

SOUPE AU PISTOU

This colourful vegetable soup from Provence is lifted with the sunny flavours of garlic, basil and golden olive oil – pounded together to a pistou or paste like the Italian pesto. Although not so colourful, it is delicious reheated and eaten the next day once the flavours have had time to meld. The variations are endless – simply use whatever vegetables are in season.

SERVES 6-8

125 g (4 oz) dried haricot,
   navy or black-eyed beans
1 onion
1 leek
2 carrots
175 g (6 oz) potatoes
350 g (12 oz) courgettes
450 g (1 lb) ripe tomatoes
125 g (4 oz) green beans
125 g (4 oz) fresh shelled
   peas (optional)
45 ml (3 tbsp) olive oil
few fresh thyme sprigs
2 bay leaves
75 g (3 oz) dried vermicelli
salt and pepper
PISTOU
25 g (1 oz) fresh basil leaves
4 garlic cloves
50 g (2 oz) freshly grated
   Parmesan cheese
150 ml (¼ pint) extra-virgin
   olive oil
TO SERVE
freshly grated Parmesan or
   Gruyère cheese

PREPARATION TIME
30 minutes, plus overnight
soaking
COOKING TIME
About 1¾ hour
FREEZING Not suitable

480-360 CALS PER SERVING

1. Place the beans in a bowl, cover with plenty of cold water and leave to soak overnight. The next day, drain the beans and transfer to a saucepan. Cover with cold water and bring to the boil. Boil steadily for 10 minutes, then lower the heat, cover and simmer for about 45 minutes to 1 hour until almost tender. Drain.

2. Peel and slice the onion; thinly slice the leek. Peel and finely dice the carrots and potatoes; dice the courgettes. Plunge the tomatoes into boiling water for 30 seconds, then remove, peel away the skins and dice the flesh. Cut the green beans into short lengths.

3. Heat the oil in a large pan, add the onion and leek and cook gently for 10 minutes until beginning to soften. Add the cooked dried beans, carrots, potatoes and herbs. Pour in enough water to cover, about 1.2 litres (2 pints). Bring to the boil, cover and simmer for 30 minutes until the white beans begin to disintegrate.

4. Meanwhile, make the pistou. Pound the basil, garlic and Parmesan in a pestle and mortar until paste-like, then gradually work in the olive oil, until amalgamated. Add salt and pepper to taste. Serve from the mortar. (Alternatively, work the basil, garlic

and Parmesan in a food processor until smooth then, with the motor running, add the olive oil in a steady stream through the feeder tube. Transfer to a bowl to serve.)

5. Add the green beans, courgettes, peas if using, tomatoes and broken vermicelli to the soup. Season with salt and pepper. Cook for a further 10-15 minutes, until all the vegetables and pasta are very tender. Check the seasoning.

6. Ladle the soup into warmed bowls and serve piping hot, accompanied by the pistou and grated cheese. Each guest stirs some pistou into their soup and adds a sprinkling of cheese.

TECHNIQUE

For the pistou, pound the basil, garlic and Parmesan together to a paste, using a pestle and mortar.

GARLIC AND ONION SOUP

This simple and delicious soup originates from South West France where it is known as *tourin*. The village of St Clar in that region has two garlic festivals in August. This soup is made by the local farmers' wives and served to all-comers in the arcaded village square at the beginning of the festivities.

SERVES 6

125 g (4 oz) plump garlic cloves

450 g (1 lb) mild onions

50 g (2 oz) duck or goose fat, or butter

15 ml (1 tbsp) plain white flour

1.4 litres (2½ pints) duck or chicken stock

2 eggs, separated

15 ml (1 tbsp) wine vinegar

salt and pepper

45 ml (3 tbsp) chopped fresh chives

6 thick slices rustic bread

PREPARATION TIME
30 minutes
COOKING TIME
About 1 hour
FREEZING
Suitable

290 CALS PER SERVING

1. Peel the garlic, place in a pan of cold water and bring to the boil, then drain. Repeat twice more, then slice the garlic. Peel and finely slice the onions.

2. Melt the duck or goose fat, or butter, in a large heavy-based saucepan and add the garlic and onions. Cook gently for about 20 minutes, stirring occasionally, until soft and golden but not coloured. Stir in the flour, cook for 1 minute, then add the stock, stirring. Bring to the boil, lower the heat and simmer for 40 minutes.

3. Stir the egg yolks and vinegar together in a bowl. Lightly beat the egg whites in another bowl to break them up.

4. Taste the soup and season liberally. Bring to boiling point and add the egg whites in a steady stream, stirring constantly. Remove from the heat and stir in the egg yolks and most of the chives.

5. Place a slice of bread in each warmed soup bowl and pour on the soup. Serve piping hot, sprinkled with the rest of the chives.

NOTE: Duck or goose fat gives this soup a rich authentic flavour and can be bought in jars and cans from delicatessens. Alternatively you can use butter, or render duck fat yourself. Simply cut skin and excess fat from a raw duck into small pieces. Place in a saucepan with 50 ml (2 fl oz) cold water and bring to the boil. Turn down the heat and simmer very slowly for 1½-2 hours. Strain through a fine sieve into a clean jar; cool, cover and store in the refrigerator until required.

VARIATIONS

• Use half leeks and half onions as the soup base.
• Stir 175 g (6 oz) blanched chopped sorrel or spinach into the soup before serving.

TECHNIQUE

Bring the soup to boiling point, then add the egg whites in a steady stream, stirring constantly, to form thin threads.

MOUCLADE

This mussel stew comes from the Vendée on the west coast, where it is traditional to farm mussels – known locally as *moucles*. Saffron imparts a delicate spicy flavour, while cream, butter and eggs enrich the dish. Serve with crusty bread to mop up the delicious juices ... and something light to follow!

SERVES 6

2.7 kg (6 lb) mussels in shells

3 shallots

200 ml (7 fl oz) dry white
    wine

large pinch of saffron
    threads

3 garlic cloves, peeled

50 g (2 oz) butter

10 ml (2 tsp) potato flour or
    cornflour

450 ml (¾ pint) double
    cream or crème fraîche

juice of 1 lemon, to taste

salt and pepper

2 egg yolks

chopped parsley or chervil,
    to garnish

PREPARATION TIME
45 minutes, plus soaking
COOKING TIME
About 20 minutes
FREEZING
Not suitable

520 CALS PER SERVING

1. Scrub the mussels thoroughly and rinse well under cold water. Pull away any 'beards', then place in a large bowl. Cover with cold water and leave to soak for at least 30 minutes to plump up the mussels. After soaking, tap the opened ones sharply with the back of a knife and discard any that do not close straight away.

2. Peel and finely chop the shallots. Place the drained mussels in a large saucepan. Add the wine and shallots. Cover tightly and cook over a high heat, shaking the pan frequently, for 5-10 minutes until the mussels are steamed open. Any that have not opened at this stage should be discarded.

3. Drain the mussels, reserving the liquid to make the sauce. Remove the empty half-shells. Return the mussels in their half-shells to the pan and cover with a lid to keep warm.

4. Put the reserved liquid in a small pan with the saffron. Bring to the boil and boil rapidly until the liquid is reduced by half. Meanwhile, finely chop the garlic.

5. Melt the butter in a small saucepan, add the garlic and cook until golden. Pour in the reduced cooking liquid. Mix the potato flour or cornflour with 45 ml (3 tbsp) water and whisk into the liquid with the cream. Bring to the boil, whisking continuously, and simmer until slightly thickened. Add lemon juice to taste, season well and stir in the egg yolks. Cook gently for 5 minutes until the sauce has thickened slightly; it should be the consistency of a pouring custard. Do not allow to boil or it may curdle.

6. Divide the mussels between warmed shallow bowls, neatly piling them on top of each other. Pour the sauce liberally over the mussels and sprinkle with parsley or chervil. Serve immediately, with plenty of bread.

VARIATION

For a quick dish, use thawed frozen cooked mussels, and fresh fish stock – available from larger supermarkets.

TECHNIQUE

Scrub the mussels thoroughly under cold running water to remove any grit and barnacles.

CHICKEN AND DUCK LIVER TERRINE

This exceptionally smooth, creamy liver terrine makes a passing alternative to *terrine de fois gras* for those who don't approve! It is served sliced with warm toast, sweet/sour caramelised onions and a glistening sweet wine jelly. The onions are equally delicious hot or cold.

SERVES 4-6

225 g (8 oz) chicken livers
225 g (8 oz) duck livers
2 shallots
150 g (5 oz) butter, softened
90 ml (3 fl oz) cognac,
    armagnac or Madeira
90 ml (3 fl oz) double cream
    or crème fraîche
salt and pepper
large pinch each of ground
    mace and allspice
WINE JELLY
300 ml (½ pint) sweet white
    wine, such as Sauternes
15 ml (1 tbsp) powdered
    gelatine
ONION MARMALADE
700 g (1½ lb) red onions
125 g (4 oz) butter
120 ml (4 fl oz) sherry or
    wine vinegar
150 g (5 oz) caster sugar
45 ml (3 tbsp) crème de
    cassis
300 ml (½ pint) full-bodied
    dry red wine

PREPARATION TIME
40 minutes, plus chilling
COOKING TIME
About 50 minutes
FREEZING Not suitable

1140 - 760 CALS PER SERVING

1. Line a 450 g (1 pint) loaf tin with cling film. Trim the chicken and duck livers, discarding any white fibrous parts and greenish discoloured bits. Peel and chop the shallots.

2. Melt 25 g (1 oz) butter in a frying pan, add the shallots and cook gently for 1-2 minutes until beginning to soften. Increase the heat slightly and add the livers. Turn them in the pan for 2-3 minutes until just 'seized', but still soft and pink on the inside. Transfer to a blender.

3. Deglaze the pan with the alcohol, scraping up any sediment. Boil to reduce by half, then transfer to the blender. Add the cream, plenty of seasoning, and the spices. Blend until smooth. Add the remaining softened butter and work again until smooth.

4. Pass the mixture through a fine sieve and check the seasoning. Spoon into the prepared tin and level the surface. Cool, then refrigerate for several hours or overnight until firm.

5. Meanwhile, make the wine jelly. Pour the wine into a small pan and sprinkle over the gelatine. Stir over a low heat to dissolve, then pour into an ice cube tray and leave to set.

6. To make the onion marmalade, peel and slice the onions. Melt the butter in a pan, add the onions with the vinegar and simmer, covered, for 10 minutes until soft. Add the sugar, turn up the heat and cook, stirring, until the onions start to caramelise and the liquid has evaporated. Add the cassis and wine, and cook gently, uncovered, for 20 minutes until all the liquid has evaporated. Season to taste.

7. To serve, turn out the terrine and cut into slices, using a warm knife. Turn out the jelly onto damp grease-proof paper and cut into cubes, using a wet knife. Serve the terrine accompanied by warm toast, the wine jelly and a spoonful of onion marmalade.

TECHNIQUE

Stir-fry the livers for 2-3 minutes until evenly browned but still pink and soft inside.

ASPARAGUS WITH POACHED EGGS

Fresh asparagus in season is not to be missed! During April and May French markets are full to brimming with inexpensive bundles of all kinds of asparagus, from fine sprue to plump white asparagus. New potatoes, poached eggs and tarragon are natural partners in this simple taste of Spring.

SERVES 6

900 g (2 lb) asparagus
salt and pepper
700 g (1 1/2 lb) small new
   potatoes, scrubbed
300 ml (1/2 pint) crème
   fraîche or whipped double
   cream
45 ml (3 tbsp) tarragon
   vinegar
45 ml (3 tbsp) chopped fresh
   tarragon
6 eggs, size 4, refrigerated
tarragon sprigs, to garnish

PREPARATION TIME
20 minutes
COOKING TIME
About 40 minutes
FREEZING
Not suitable

400 CALS PER SERVING

1. Peel the tough skin from the lower end of the asparagus stalks, using a swivel potato peeler. Trim the stalks to an even length.

2. Fill a roasting tin with cold water and add salt. Bring to the boil and lay the asparagus in the tin. Boil for 10-15 minutes or longer, depending on the variety and thickness of the stalks. Test with a knife after 10 minutes, then at 5 minute intervals (see technique).

3. Lift the asparagus out of the roasting tin and immediately plunge into a bowl of cold water to set the colour and stop the cooking. Set aside.

4. Pour the asparagus water into a saucepan, add the potatoes and cook for 15-20 minutes until tender. Using a slotted spoon, transfer the potatoes to a colander and cool slightly. Reserve the water for poaching the eggs.

5. Mix the crème fraîche with 15 ml (1 tbsp) vinegar. Stir in the tarragon, season, cover and refrigerate.

6. Slice the potatoes and arrange on serving plates. Season well. Drain and dry the asparagus on kitchen paper and lay over the potatoes.

7. Bring the reserved asparagus water to a rolling boil in a large shallow pan, adding the remaining 30 ml (2 tbsp) vinegar and more water if necessary. Break the eggs into the bubbling water, then turn down to a bare simmer. Poach for about 4 minutes or longer – ideally they should still be quite soft. Lift out, drain on kitchen paper and arrange on the asparagus. Season and serve at once, with the tarragon cream.

VARIATIONS

• Use quail's eggs, allowing two per person; poach for 1 minute only.
• Flavour the cream with chopped chervil instead of tarragon.

TECHNIQUE

To test the asparagus, pierce the lower part of the stalk with a sharp knife. If there isn't much resistance it is ready.

SALAD OF BAYONNE HAM, MELON AND ARTICHOKES

In France, country or mountain hams are dried and sometimes smoked too. They are typically served in thick slices as part of a salad or *assiette de charcuterie*. Here the classic combination of salty ham and sweet juicy melon is enhanced with tender young artichoke hearts and a herb vinaigrette.

SERVES 6

12 fresh baby artichokes
   (see note)
lemon juice, for brushing
30 ml (2 tbsp) olive oil
salt and pepper
1 ripe orange-fleshed
   melon, such as
   Charantais or Cantaloupe
6 thick slices Bayonne or
   Parma ham
HERB VINAIGRETTE
15 ml (1 tbsp) red wine
   vinegar
5 ml (1 tsp) Dijon mustard
45 ml (3 tbsp) olive oil
15 ml (1 tbsp) chopped
   fresh chervil or tarragon
TO SERVE
salad leaves
herb sprigs, to garnish

PREPARATION TIME
35 minutes
COOKING TIME
10 minutes
FREEZING
Not suitable

180 CALS PER SERVING

1. To prepare the artichokes, break off the tough outer leaves at the base until you expose a central core of pale leaves. Slice off the tough green or purple tips. Using a small sharp knife, pare the dark green skin from the base and down the stem. Brush the cut parts with lemon juice to prevent browning. Cut into quarters and brush with lemon juice.

2. Heat the oil in a sauté pan or heavy-based frying pan. Add the artichokes and cook over a high heat, stirring constantly, until they are just turning brown. Transfer to a bowl and allow to cool. Season with salt and pepper.

3. Halve the melon and scoop out the seeds. Either scoop the flesh into balls, cut into cubes or skin and slice thinly. Place the melon in the bowl with the artichokes. Toss lightly to mix.

4. Whisk all the ingredients for the dressing together until evenly amalgamated. Season with salt and pepper to taste. Pour over the artichokes and melon and turn to coat.

5. Using a sharp knife, slice the ham into finger-like strips and add to the melon and artichokes.

6. Arrange a few salad leaves on each individual serving plate and spoon the salad on top. Garnish with herb sprigs and serve immediately.

NOTE: Be sure to choose a fully ripe melon. A sweet, perfumed aroma is the best indicator of ripeness. Other varieties of melon can be substituted.

If fresh baby artichokes are unobtainable, use 12 frozen prepared artichoke hearts instead. Defrost thoroughly before use.

VARIATIONS

Replace the Bayonne ham with sliced dried smoked duck breast, or even Italian bresaola (cured beef).

TECHNIQUE

Using a small sharp knife, pare the dark green skin from the base and stems of the baby artichokes, working downwards.

SQUID WITH RAITO

Raito is a classic red wine and tomato sauce flavoured with garlic, herbs, capers and olives, from Provence. It is traditionally served with white fish, such as hake or whiting and salt cod, at festivals.

SERVES 4

900 g (2 lb) small squid
RAITO
1 large onion
2-3 garlic cloves
450 g (1 lb) ripe tomatoes
   (see note)
50 g (2 oz) walnuts (optional)
45 ml (3 tbsp) olive oil
30 ml (2 tbsp) flour
450 ml (¾ pint) red wine
30 ml (2 tbsp) sun-dried
   tomato paste or tomato
   purée
1 bay leaf
5 ml (1 tsp) dried thyme
2.5 ml (½ tsp) dried
   rosemary
2.5 ml (½ tsp) fennel seed
pinch of ground cloves
salt and pepper
5 ml (1 tsp) sugar (optional)
50 g (2 oz) capers
16 small black olives
   (preferably Niçoise)
60 ml (4 tbsp) chopped fresh
   parsley
TO GARNISH
parsley sprigs

PREPARATION TIME
20 minutes
COOKING TIME
About 1½ hours
FREEZING
Suitable: Sauce only

540 CALS PER SERVING

1. First make the raito. Peel and chop the onion and garlic. Roughly chop the tomatoes. Finely grind the walnuts, if using.

2. Heat the oil in a flameproof casserole, add the onion and garlic and cook gently for 15-20 minutes, until very soft but not coloured.

3. Stir in the flour. Gradually stir in the red wine and 450 ml (¾ pint) boiling water. Add the tomatoes, tomato purée, walnuts if using, bay leaf, thyme, rosemary, fennel and cloves. Bring to a fast simmer and cook, uncovered, for about 1½ hours until reduced to 750 ml (1¼ pints).

4. Meanwhile, prepare the squid. Firmly pull the tentacles from the body pouch, making sure the soft innards come out too. Cut the head from the tentacles just in front of the eyes, reserving the tentacles. Pull out the thin transparent quill from the body and discard. Leave the body pouch and tentacles whole.

5. Taste and season the raito sauce with salt, pepper and a little sugar if necessary. Purée in a blender or food processor, then sieve to remove the tomato seeds.

6. Reheat, then stir in the drained and rinsed capers, together with half of the olives and parsley.

7. Preheat a cast-iron griddle until searing hot. Add the squid and cook for 2 minutes on each side. Spoon some of the sauce onto warmed individual serving plates and pile the squid on top. Scatter over the remaining parsley and olives. Serve at once, garnished with parsley.

NOTE: For optimum flavour make sure you use ripe, flavourful tomatoes. If unobtainable, use a 400 g (14 oz) can chopped tomatoes instead.

VARIATION

Replace the squid with 900 g (2 lb) whiting, hake or cod fillet, cut into large cubes. Toss in flour and shallow-fry in olive oil for 2-3 minutes until barely cooked. Drain on kitchen paper, then add to the raito and simmer for 5 minutes.

TECHNIQUE

Cook the squid on a searing hot cast-iron griddle for 2 minutes each side, turning once.

MOULES FRITES

There is nothing quite like sitting down to a bowl of plump mussels fried to a golden crunch in butter and breadcrumbs, thin crisp *pommes frites* and a bowl of aïoli – singing with garlic!

SERVES 4-6

2.3 kg (5 lb) mussels in
   shells, or 900 g (2 lb)
   cooked shelled mussels

3 egg yolks

I egg white

salt and pepper

175 - 225 g (6 - 8 oz) fresh
   white breadcrumbs

900 g (2 lb) potatoes, such
   as Désirée, King Edward,
   Maris Piper

oil for deep-frying

225 g (8 oz) butter

AIOLI

8 large garlic cloves

2 egg yolks

about 450 ml (¾ pint) light
   olive oil (preferably
   Provençal)

squeeze of lemon juice, to
   taste

TO GARNISH

lemon wedges

PREPARATION TIME
45 minutes, plus soaking
COOKING TIME
About 30 minutes
FREEZING
Not suitable

1600-1100 CALS PER SERVING

1. Clean the mussels thoroughly under cold running water and pull away any 'beards'. Soak in a bowl, of cold water for at least 30 minutes.

2. Meanwhile, make the aïoli. Put the garlic and egg yolks in a blender or food processor with a pinch of salt and blend until smooth. With the motor running, pour in half of the oil in a thin steady stream until the mixture starts to thicken. Add lemon juice and add the rest of the oil more boldly until it is all incorporated and the aïoli is thick. Check the seasoning. Set aside in a cool place, not the refrigerator.

3. After soaking, drain the mussels and tap each opened one sharply with the back of a knife; discard any that do not close. Place the mussels in a large saucepan with 300 ml (½ pint) water. Cover tightly and cook over a high heat, shaking the pan frequently for 5-8 minutes until the mussels open; do not overcook. Drain, discarding any unopened ones. Remove the mussels from their shells and pat dry.

4. Beat the egg yolks and white together in a bowl with a little salt, then add the mussels and toss to coat. Spread the breadcrumbs out on a tray and roll the mussels in them to coat evenly. Chill in the refrigerator.

5. Peel the potatoes and cut into 5 mm (¼ inch) slices. Stack 3-4 slices on top of each other, cut into thin chips, then immerse in a bowl of cold water. Repeat with the remaining potatoes. Rinse well, drain and pat very dry.

6. Half-fill a deep-fat fryer (with chip basket) with oil and heat to 150°C (300°F). Fry the potatoes in small batches for 4-7 minutes depending on thickness, until tender, but not coloured. Lift out and drain.

7. Melt half the butter in a large frying pan. When foaming, quickly fry half the mussels until golden brown, transfer to a warmed plate, while frying the rest.

8. Meanwhile, raise the temperature of the oil to 185°C (360°F) and fry the potatoes for a further 30 seconds - 2 minutes until golden brown and crisp. Drain on kitchen paper and sprinkle with salt. Serve immediately, with the mussels, aïoli and lemon wedges.

TECHNIQUE

Clean the mussels thoroughly, scraping away any barnacles.

Seafood Matelote

This particular *matelote de fruits de mer* is a delicate fish stew of monkfish, scallops and prawns in a creamy sauce, slightly thickened by potatoes. The inclusion of curry may not seem French, but it is, as spices were imported into France by traders from the Orient many years ago.

SERVES 6

450 g (1 lb) filleted monkfish tail

225 g (8 oz) shelled scallops

525 g (1¼ lb) raw prawns in shell

6 shallots

2 fennel bulbs

150 g (5 oz) butter

1.5 kg (3 lb) potatoes

15 ml (1 tbsp) curry paste

450 ml (¾ pint) fish stock

300 ml (½ pint) crème fraîche or double cream

45 ml (3 tbsp) flour

2 ripe tomatoes

salt and pepper

squeeze of lemon juice (optional)

TAPENADE

175 g (6 oz) black olives, pitted

2 garlic cloves, peeled

3 canned anchovies, drained

10 ml (2 tsp) capers, drained

15 ml (1 tbsp) olive oil

TO SERVE

1 small thin French stick

fennel sprigs, to garnish

PREPARATION TIME
35 minutes
COOKING TIME
About 40 minutes
FREEZING Not suitable

825 CALS PER SERVING

1. Preheat the oven to 180°C (350°F) Mark 4. Cut the monkfish into bite-sized chunks. Trim the scallops if necessary, but leave whole. Peel the prawns, leaving the tail end attached. Cover and refrigerate.

2. Peel and finely chop the shallots. Trim, quarter and core the fennel, then slice thickly.

3. Melt 75 g (3 oz) butter in a frying pan, add the shallots and cook gently for 5 minutes until beginning to soften. Meanwhile, peel and roughly dice the potatoes. Add to the pan and cook for 4-5 minutes until they start to soften. Transfer the potatoes and shallots to a casserole.

4. Add the fennel to the butter remaining in the pan, increase the heat and cook for a few minutes until just turning brown; add to the casserole.

5. Add the curry paste to the pan and cook for 1 minute, scraping up any residue. Pour in the stock and cream, stirring. Bring to the boil and pour over the vegetables in the casserole. Cover and cook in the oven for 15 minutes.

6. Toss the monkfish, scallops and prawns in the flour. Melt the remaining butter in the frying pan and fry the seafood in batches quickly until golden.

Add to the casserole and cook for a further 10-15 minutes until the potatoes and fish are tender.

7. Meanwhile, put all the ingredients for the tapenade into a food processor and blend until smooth.

8. In the meantime, skin, deseed and thinly slice the tomatoes, then stir into the matelote. Check the seasoning and add a little lemon juice if necessary.

9. Cut the French bread into 12 very thin slices, toast on both sides and spread thinly with the tapenade. Serve the matelote, garnished with fennel and accompanied by the tapenade toasts.

NOTE: For a less rich version, use 150 ml (¼ pint) cream and 600 ml (1 pint) fish stock.

TECHNIQUE

Peel the prawns, leaving the fan-shaped tail end shell intact.

SEARED COD WITH WILTED SPINACH

Thick fillets of the freshest cod are quickly pan-fried to crisp the skin, then roasted briefly in the oven until just firm and juicy. Served on a bed of bright green buttery spinach with a creamy light beurre blanc sauce, this is a sophisticated dish, full of contrasting flavours and textures.

SERVES 4

4 thick pieces cod fillet, with
  skin, each about 175 g
  (6 oz)
flour, for coating
salt and pepper
30 ml (2 tbsp) olive oil
900 g (2 lb) spinach
50 g (2 oz) butter
BEURRE BLANC
2 shallots, skinned and finely
  diced
45 ml (3 tbsp) white wine
45 ml (3 tbsp) white wine
  vinegar
15 ml (1 tbsp) double cream
250 g (8 oz) unsalted butter,
  chilled and cubed
squeeze of lemon juice
30 ml (2 tbsp) chopped fresh
  chives

PREPARATION TIME
35 minutes
COOKING TIME
15 minutes
FREEZING
Not suitable

840 CALS PER SERVING

1. Preheat the oven to 200°C (400°F) Mark 6. Roll the cod in the flour to coat and season with pepper. Heat the olive oil in a heavy-based frying pan over high heat until almost smoking. Add the fish, skin-side down, and cook for 2 minutes, then place in a baking tin, skin-side up, and set aside.

2. Remove the tough stalks from the spinach, then wash well. Spin-dry in a salad basket or dry on kitchen paper. Melt the butter in a large saucepan, add the spinach and cook over a high heat until just wilted. Remove from the heat and season well.

3. Roast the cod for 8 minutes or until just opaque and cooked. Rest in a warm place for 5 minutes while making the sauce.

4. Meanwhile peel and finely dice the shallots. Place in a small pan with the wine, vinegar and 45 ml (3 tbsp) water. Boil until reduced to 15 ml (1 tbsp), stir in the cream and reduce again.

5. Over a low heat, gradually whisk in butter, piece by piece, until amalgamated; this process shouldn't take too long. Do not allow to boil or become too hot or the sauce will split; if necessary remove from the heat as you whisk in more butter. Add lemon juice, salt and pepper to taste, and stir in chives.

6. Reheat the spinach, pile onto warmed serving plates, top with a piece of roast cod and pour over the sauce. Serve immediately.

NOTE: For optimum flavour and texture, it is essential to use very fresh fish for this recipe.

VARIATION

Replace the spinach with 450 g (1 lb) sliced leeks, sautéed in butter, or blanched and grilled baby leeks.

TECHNIQUE

For the beurre blanc, whisk in the butter a piece at a time, until creamy and amalgamated.

TUNA STEAKS À LA GRUISSON WITH PIPÉRADE

During August, the tuna fishermen from Gruisson in South West France cook an extraordinary open-air meal for some 300 people at the St Clar Garlic Festival. This is my version of their way of cooking tuna steaks, though they cook them over wood embers in converted halved oil drums! The pipérade is my own addition.

SERVES 4

4 red tuna steaks, each 2.5 cm (1 inch) thick
olive oil, for basting
MUSTARD MARINADE
4 garlic cloves, crushed
60 ml (4 tbsp) Dijon mustard
30 ml (2 tbsp) armagnac
salt and pepper
PIPERADE
900 g (2 lb) ripe flavourful tomatoes, or two 400 g (14 oz) cans chopped tomatoes
90 ml (6 tbsp) olive oil
10 ml (2 tsp) harissa (see note)
2 onions
3 garlic cloves
3 large red peppers

PREPARATION TIME
30 minutes, plus marinating
COOKING TIME
1¼ hours
FREEZING
Suitable: Pipérade only

645 CALS PER SERVING

1. For the mustard marinade, mix the crushed garlic with the mustard, armagnac and salt and pepper to taste. Spread over the cut sides of the tuna. Lay in a non-metal dish, cover and leave to marinate in a cool place for about 1 hour.

2. To make the pipérade, immerse the fresh tomatoes in boiling water for 30 seconds, then remove and peel away the skins. Halve, deseed and chop the tomatoes. Heat 45 ml (3 tbsp) oil in a saucepan, add the harissa and cook, stirring, for 1 minute. Add the tomatoes and cook gently for about 10 minutes until pulpy.

3. Peel and chop the onions and garlic. Halve, core and deseed the peppers, then cut into thin strips. Heat the remaining oil in a frying pan and sauté the onions, garlic and peppers for about 10 minutes until beginning to soften. Add the pepper mixture to the tomato and simmer, covered, for 1 hour until very soft. Season with salt and pepper to taste.

4. Preheat the grill. Drizzle the tuna steaks with olive oil and arrange on a foil-lined grill pan. Grill for about 5 minutes on each side until crusty on the outside and still pink in the middle. Alternatively cook on a barbecue, allowing a little less time. Accompany with the pipérade, which may be served hot or cold.

NOTE: Harissa is an aromatic spicy paste from North Africa, which is often used in the cooking of southern France. It is available here, from delicatessens and Indian food stores. If unobtainable substitute 15 ml (1 tbsp) tomato purée mixed with a little crushed garlic, paprika and cayenne to taste.

VARIATION

Use a mixture of green, yellow and red peppers for the pipérade.

TECHNIQUE

Spread the mustard marinade over the cut surfaces of the tuna steaks.

QUENELLES AU GRATIN

Robust puffs of herby fish mousseline are poached, then coated in a light cheese sauce and grilled until golden brown and crisp on top. This recipe uses an easy method for shaping quenelles.

SERVES 4

CHOUX PASTRY
110 g (4 oz) plain flour
5 ml (1 tsp) salt
50 g (2 oz) butter, cubed
2 eggs

FISH PASTE
550 g (1¼ lb) filleted,
    skinned whiting or pollack
salt and pepper
60 ml (4 tbsp) double
    cream, chilled
30 ml (2 tbsp) chopped
    mixed herbs, such as
    chervil, tarragon and
    chives

CHEESE SAUCE
75 g (3 oz) butter
50 g (2 oz) plain flour
2.5 ml (½ tsp) paprika
300 ml (½ pint) milk
150 ml (¼ pint) fish stock
150 ml (¼ pint) white wine
150 ml (¼ pint) crème
    fraîche or double cream
125 g (4 oz) Gruyère cheese,
    grated
squeeze of lemon juice
    (optional)

PREPARATION TIME
30 minutes
COOKING TIME
30 minutes
FREEZING
Not suitable

1125 CALS PER SERVING

1. To make the choux pastry, sift the flour onto a sheet of greaseproof paper. Put 300 ml (½ pint) water in a saucepan with the salt and butter and heat slowly. Once the butter has melted, bring to a rolling boil, and tip in the flour all at once. Remove from the heat and beat vigorously until the mixture comes together and leaves the sides of the pan. Let cool for 1 minute, then gradually add the eggs, beating well after each addition, until the mixture is shiny but quite stiff. You may not need all of the egg. Set aside.

2. To prepare the fish paste, place the fish in a food processor and blend until smooth. Season with salt and pepper. Using an electric beater, beat the fish paste into the choux paste until smooth. Cover and chill in the refrigerator for at least 1 hour.

3. Whisk in the chilled cream, a little at a time, until the mixture will just drop off a wooden spoon, but hold its shape. Stir in the herbs. Chill.

4. To make the sauce, melt two thirds of the butter in a saucepan and stir in the flour and paprika. Cook over a low heat for 1-2 minutes, then gradually whisk in the milk, stock and wine. Slowly bring to the boil and simmer for 5 minutes. Stir in the cream and half of the cheese. Add seasoning and lemon juice to taste. Pour half the sauce into a shallow buttered baking dish.

5. Bring a 7.5 cm (3 inch) depth of water or fish stock to the boil in a large, wide pan. Lower the heat until the liquid is barely simmering. Scoop 16 rough balls of quenelle mixture onto a wet plate or tray. Poach the quenelles in batches, for 15 to 20 minutes until doubled in size. Drain on kitchen paper and place on top of the cheese sauce.

6. Preheat the grill. Spoon the remaining sauce over the quenelles and sprinkle with the reserved cheese. Dot with the remaining butter and grill for 10-15 minutes until heated through and well browned.

VARIATIONS

• Use salmon instead of white fish.
• Stir 125 g (4 oz) chopped peeled prawns into the fish paste.

TECHNIQUE

Poach the quenelles in the barely simmering liquid for 15-20 minutes until doubled in size. Drain on kitchen paper.

COQ AU VIN BLANC

For this traditional recipe an old cockerel which needed long slow cooking was once always used, but this is a lighter, quicker version. Buy a good quality chicken to ensure the casserole has maximum flavour. Using white wine rather than red makes the dish lighter and less wintery. The sauce is brimming with mushrooms and onions, which are added at the last moment to keep them firm. If you have time to make some, fresh herb-flavoured noodles make an ideal accompaniment.

SERVES 4-6

1 corn-fed or free-range chicken, weighing about 1.4 kg (3 lb), jointed
1 bottle full-bodied white wine, such as Burgundy or Chardonnay
60 ml (4 tbsp) brandy
2 bay leaves
2 bouquet garnis
few sprigs of fresh thyme
1 garlic clove, peeled and bruised
seasoned flour, for coating
125 g (4 oz) butter
125 g (4 oz) piece unsmoked bacon
225 g (8 oz) pickling onions
225 g (8 oz) brown cap mushrooms
salt and pepper
BEURRE MANIE
50 g (2 oz) butter, softened
30 ml (2 tbsp) flour

PREPARATION TIME
45 minutes
COOKING TIME
45 minutes
FREEZING
Suitable

865-580 CALS PER SERVING

1. Pour the wine and brandy into a saucepan and add the bay leaves, 1 bouquet garni, the thyme sprigs and garlic. Bring to the boil and simmer until reduced by half. Allow to cool.

2. Toss the chicken in a little seasoned flour. Melt half of the butter in a large frying pan. When foaming, add the chicken joints and brown all over, then transfer to a flameproof casserole. Cut the bacon into lardons, add to the frying pan and fry until golden. Remove with a slotted spoon and add to the chicken.

3. Strain the cooled reduced wine mixture over the chicken and add the other bouquet garni. Bring to the boil, lower the heat, cover and simmer very slowly for 30 minutes.

4. Meanwhile, peel the onions but leave the root ends intact. Halve or quarter the mushrooms if large. Melt the butter in a frying pan, add the onions and fry until tender and lightly browned. Add the mushrooms and fry until softened. Add the mushrooms and onions to the casserole, cover and cook for a further 10 minutes or until the chicken is tender.

5. For the beurre manié, work the butter and flour together to a paste.

6. Lift out the chicken and vegetables and place in a warmed serving dish; cover and keep warm. Bring the cooking liquid in the casserole to the boil. Whisk in the beurre manié, a piece at a time, until the sauce is shiny and syrupy. Taste and adjust the seasoning. Pour the sauce over the chicken to serve.

NOTE: If preferred, cook the casserole in the oven at 180°C (350°F) Mark 4.

TECHNIQUE

Fry the chicken joints in the butter, turning frequently, until evenly browned.

GRILLED DUCK BREAST WITH MAIZE 'CHIPS'

Bouillie is a maize meal porridge from Perigord, which is traditionally served with soup or stews. Here it is cooled and set, then cut into 'chips' and fried until golden. Crunchy on the outside, but soft in the middle, they are the ideal complement to succulent grilled duck breast fillets.

SERVES 4

2 large boneless duck
    breasts, each 350 g (12 oz)
DRY MARINADE
2 garlic cloves
1 shallot
10 ml (2 tsp) sea salt
10 ml (2 tsp) fines herbes
5 ml (1 tsp) black
    peppercorns, crushed
BOUILLIE
50 g (2 oz) butter or duck
    fat
salt and pepper
125 g (4 oz) maize meal
    (fine polenta)
oil for deep-frying
SAUCE
250 ml (8 fl oz) sherry
    vinegar
45 ml (3 tbsp) sugar
300 ml (1/2 pint) strong duck
    or game stock
150 ml (1/4 pint) double
    cream

PREPARATION TIME
25 minutes, plus overnight
marinating
COOKING TIME
45 minutes
FREEZING Not suitable

925 CALS PER SERVING

1. For the dry marinade, peel and finely chop the garlic and shallot. Mix with the rest of the marinade ingredients, then rub all over the duck breasts. Place, skin-side down, in a non-metallic dish. Cover and leave to marinate in the refrigerator overnight, turning once.

2. To make the bouillie, put the butter or duck fat in a saucepan with 600 ml (1 pint) water and bring to the boil. Shower in the maize meal, whisking all the time. Cook, stirring constantly, for 15 minutes or until the mixture leaves the sides of the pan. Add seasoning. Turn into a shallow oiled dish, smooth the top, cool, then chill until firm.

3. Lift the duck breasts out of the marinade and pat dry with kitchen paper. Lightly score the skin with a sharp knife. Allow to come to room temperature.

4. For the sauce, put the vinegar and sugar into a small heavy-based pan and heat gently until dissolved. Bring to the boil and boil rapidly to a deep caramel. Immediately pour in the stock and bring to the boil. Add the cream and boil for 5 minutes until syrupy. Season with pepper to taste. Keep warm.

5. Turn out the bouillie and cut into thick chips. Roll in a little flour. Heat the oil for deep-frying to 180°C (350°F). Deep-fry the chips in batches for 6-8 minutes until golden brown and crisp. Drain on kitchen paper and keep warm in a low oven with the door ajar.

6. Preheat the grill. Place the duck breasts, skin-side down, on a grill rack. Grill about 10 cm (4 inches) from the element for 3 minutes to seal. Turn and grill for about 8-10 minutes until medium-rare. Test by piercing with a sharp knife; the juices should be pink. Let rest for 3 minutes before slicing.

7. Reheat the sauce. Slice the duck breasts thickly and arrange on warmed serving plates. Pour over a little sauce and serve with the "chips".

TECHNIQUE

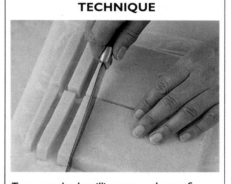

Turn out the bouillie onto a sheet of dampened paper and cut into broad chips, using a wet knife.

RABBIT WITH MUSTARD AND PRUNES

This classic dish appears on menus throughout France as *lapin au moutarde*. Here sweet, juicy prunes are complemented by the rich sharp mustard sauce too. These are pre-soaked in fruity wine to enhance flavour. Use real dried prunes which readily absorb liquid, rather than no-need-to soak ones.

SERVES 4-6

1 rabbit, weighing 1.4 kg
   (3 lb), jointed
225 g (8 oz) dried prunes
1 bottle fruity white wine
60 ml (4 tbsp) Dijon
   mustard
salt and pepper
6 shallots
50 g (2 oz) butter
15 ml (1 tbsp) chopped fresh
   thyme
300 ml ($\frac{1}{2}$ pint) crème
   fraîche or double cream
thyme sprigs, to garnish

PREPARATION TIME
25 minutes, plus overnight
soaking
COOKING TIME
1 hour
FREEZING
Not suitable

715 - 480 CALS PER SERVING

1. Put the prunes in a bowl, pour on the wine, cover and leave to soak overnight.

2. The next day, spread half of the mustard over the rabbit joints and place in a non-metallic dish. Cover and leave to marinate in a cool place for 1 hour or longer.

3. Preheat the oven to 230°C (450°F) Mark 8. Transfer the rabbit and any juices to a shallow flameproof casserole. Roast, uncovered, for 15 minutes. Drain prunes, reserving wine.

4. Lower the oven setting to 170°C (325°F) Mark 3. Lift the rabbit onto a plate and deglaze the casserole with the reserved wine. Replace the rabbit, add the prunes and season well. Bring to a simmer, cover and return to the oven for 30-40 minutes or until the rabbit is tender.

5. Meanwhile, peel and slice the shallots. Melt the butter in a small pan, add the shallots and thyme and cook gently until soft and golden.

6. Remove the rabbit and prunes from the casserole; keep warm. Boil the liquid to reduce by half, then stir in the cream and remaining mustard. Simmer for 10 minutes, then stir in the shallots. Return the rabbit and prunes to the casserole and heat thoroughly. Serve garnished with thyme.

NOTE: If a whole rabbit is unobtainable, buy the same weight of rabbit joints or 900 g (2 lb) boneless rabbit pieces. If necessary tie with cotton string.

VARIATIONS

• For a lighter version, halve the quantity of wine. At stage 4 add 375 ml (12 fl oz) chicken stock with the wine. Omit the crème fraîche and, without reducing the sauce, thicken with a beurre manié (see page 36).
• Use chicken instead of rabbit joints.

TECHNIQUE

Add the reserved wine to the casserole to deglaze, scraping up any brown sediment sticking to the base.

BOUDIN BLANC

Delicate, light sausages, perfumed with dried mushrooms, are served with creamy mashed potatoes, and sautéed apples and shallots. Most butchers sell sausage casings but – if filling sausages strikes you with terror – shape the mixture into a large sausage, wrap tightly in muslin, secure ends with string, and poach for 45 minutes-1 hour until firm. Cool overnight. Unwrap, slice thickly and fry in butter to serve.

SERVES 4-6

BOUDIN BLANC

25 g (1 oz) dried ceps or
   porcini mushrooms
150 ml (¼ pint) double
   cream
125 g (4 oz) fresh white
   breadcrumbs
2 shallots, peeled
250 g (8 oz) veal or pork
   escalope
225 g (8 oz) belly pork
225 g (8 oz) skinless chicken
   breast fillet
3 eggs, beaten
pinch of ground allspice
pinch of ground nutmeg
salt and white pepper
pork sausage casings
300 ml (½ pint) milk
TO SERVE
900 g (2 lb) floury potatoes
300 ml (½ pint) hot milk
175 g (6 oz) butter
6 spring onions, chopped
2 eating apples
lemon juice, for sprinkling
6 shallots
15 ml (1 tbsp) sugar

PREPARATION TIME
1 hour, plus soaking
COOKING TIME
30 minutes
FREEZING Not suitable

1160-775 CALS PER SERVING

1. Soak the mushrooms in boiling water to cover for 30 minutes.

2. Bring cream to the boil, pour on to the breadcrumbs and leave until cold.

3. Mince the shallots in a food processor. Cut all meats into chunks, add to the processor and work until smooth.

4. Transfer the meat to a large bowl and add the cold breadcrumb mixture, eggs and spices. Drain the mushrooms, chop finely and add to the bowl. Mix thoroughly, seasoning well.

5. To fill the casings, spoon the sausagemeat into a large piping bag, fitted with a large nozzle. Rinse the casings in cold water and roll the open end over the nozzle. Hold the first 5 cm (2 inches) closed and squeeze the filling into the casing to form the first sausage, easing the casing from the nozzle as it fills. When the sausage is big enough, twist gently. Tie the loose end of the casing. Continue until all filling is used. If you like, tie at intervals between the links, then cut into individual sausages.

6. Put the milk in a large wide pan, top up with water and heat. Poach the sausages at a bare simmer for about 20 minutes until firm. Leave to cool in the liquid, then remove. Refrigerate

for up to 2 days until ready to use.

7. Peel the potatoes and boil until soft; drain and mash. Beat in the milk; the mixture should be quite soft. Beat in 50 g (2 oz) butter, the onions and seasoning. Cover and keep warm.

8. Meanwhile, halve, core and thickly slice the apples; toss in a little lemon juice. Peel and slice the shallots. Melt 50 g (2 oz) butter in a frying pan and sauté shallots for 5 minutes; remove with a slotted spoon. Add apples and sugar to the pan and fry quickly for 4-5 minutes until starting to caramelise. Return shallots to the pan; keep warm.

9. Melt remaining butter in a frying pan and gently fry the boudins for 4-5 minutes until golden on both sides. Serve with the potatoes and apples.

TECHNIQUE

Use a large piping bag fitted with a plain nozzle to fill the sausage casings.

BRETON-STYLE LAMB

A leg of lamb studded with garlic and rosemary, then braised with haricot or black-eyed beans and cherry tomatoes makes a real family feast! The cherry tomatoes keep their shape and colour in this version, and add a delicious sharpness to the rich bean mixture.

SERVES 6-8

1 leg of lamb, weighing about 2.7 kg (6 lb)

350 g (12 oz) dried haricot, black-eyed beans or flageolets

2 onions

3 carrots

1 celery stick

1 bouquet garni

6 garlic cloves

12 small fresh rosemary sprigs (approximately)

salt and pepper

300 ml (½ pint) lamb or vegetable stock (approximately)

1 bunch spring onions

50 g (2 oz) butter

15 ml (1 tbsp) mixed chopped fresh rosemary and thyme

350 g (12 oz) ripe cherry tomatoes, halved

PREPARATION TIME
25 minutes, plus overnight soaking
COOKING TIME
About 1½-2 hours
FREEZING
Suitable: Beans only

775-580 CALS PER SERVING

1. Soak the beans in plenty of cold water overnight.

2. The next day, drain the beans and place in a large saucepan. Peel and quarter 1 onion and 1 carrot; roughly chop the celery. Add to the beans with the bouquet garni. Cover with plenty of cold water and bring to the boil. Boil steadily for 10 minutes, then lower the heat. Simmer, covered, for 1-2 hours depending on the type and age of the beans; they should be just cooked, not disintegrating.

3. Meanwhile, preheat the oven to 220°C (425°F) Mark 7. Trim any excess fat from the lamb, leaving a thin covering. Weigh the joint and calculate the cooking time, allowing 15 minutes per 450 g (1 lb) for medium; 20 minutes for well-done. Peel and slice the garlic. Make several incisions in the meat and insert the garlic and rosemary.

4. Peel and chop the remaining onion and carrots. Place the lamb in a roasting tin and surround with the chopped vegetables. Season with salt and pepper. Brown in the oven for 15 minutes, then lower the oven setting to 200°C (400°F) Mark 6. Pour on the stock and cook for the rest of the calculated time; about 1¼-1½ hours. Baste frequently with the pan juices, adding more stock if necessary.

5. Meanwhile, drain the beans, reserving the liquid but discarding the vegetables and bouquet garni. Finely chop the spring onions. Melt the butter in a saucepan and fry the onions until soft and beginning to colour. Add the beans and herbs and moisten with a little of the reserved liquid. Season well. Simmer for 5 minutes, adding extra liquid if necessary to keep the beans moist.

6. Allow the lamb to rest in a warm place for 15-20 minutes. Skim off the fat from the meat juices. Five minutes before serving, stir the cherry tomatoes and 45 ml (3 tbsp) of the meat juices into the beans and heat through.

7. Transfer the lamb to a warmed platter and surround with the beans. Strain the remaining pan juices into a gravy boat and serve with the lamb.

TECHNIQUE

Using a small sharp knife, make incisions in the meat and insert a sliver of garlic and a sprig of rosemary in each one.

CARBONNADE DE BOEUF

Thin 'steaks' of lean stewing beef are cooked with caramelised onions and beer in my version of this classic recipe. The meat is always cut into thin slices, stemming back from the days when it was grilled over charcoal or charbon, hence the name *carbonnade*.

SERVES 6

1.4 kg (3 lb) chuck or rump
    steak, in one piece
50 g (2 oz) beef dripping
700 g (1½ lb) onions
4 garlic cloves, crushed
30 ml (2 tbsp) light brown
    sugar
45 ml (3 tbsp) flour
600 ml (1 pint) light ale or
    lager
300 ml (½ pint) beef stock
    or consommé
1 bay leaf
2 large fresh thyme sprigs
salt and pepper
30 ml (2 tbsp) wine or cider
    vinegar
chopped parsley, to garnish

PREPARATION TIME
35 minutes
COOKING TIME
About 2½ hours
FREEZING
Suitable

475 CALS PER SERVING

1. Preheat the oven to 150°C (300°F) Mark 2. Trim the meat and cut into large thin 'steaks'. Heat the beef dripping in a large heavy-based frying pan or sauté pan and brown the meat in batches over a high heat. Transfer to a large casserole, using a slotted spoon.

2. Peel and halve the onions, then slice thinly. Add the onions to the dripping remaining in the pan and cook for 10 minutes, stirring until they begin to soften. Add the garlic and sugar, mix well and cook gently for 10 minutes or until they begin to brown and caramelise.

3. Stir in the flour, then gradually add the beer, stirring. Bring to the boil, scraping up any sediment from the bottom of the pan, then pour over the beef in the casserole.

4. Pour the beef stock over the meat and onions and add the herbs and plenty of pepper. Stir lightly to mix. Bring to a simmer, then cover tightly and cook in the oven for about 2 hours. Stir in the vinegar and cook for a further 30 minutes or until the meat is very tender. Check the seasoning. Serve garnished with chopped parsley and accompanied by boiled potatoes and a green vegetable.

VARIATION

For a darker stew, use half light ale and half sweet stout.

TECHNIQUE

Cook the onions with the garlic and sugar over a low heat until lightly browned and beginning to caramelise.

DAUBE DE BOEUF NIÇOISE

This famous beef and wine stew from Southern France takes its name from the casserole it is cooked in – called a *daubière*. Large chunks of lean beef are marinated in wine, then stewed slowly until meltingly soft. You will need to start preparing the daube a couple of days ahead.

SERVES 6

1.4 kg (3 lb) stewing beef,
**   such as shin or chuck**
MARINADE
2 bottles of red wine
3 onions
2 garlic cloves
2 carrots
1 celery stick
2 bay leaves
2 large fresh thyme sprigs
8 peppercorns, crushed
2 cloves
DAUBE
2 onions
2 carrots
125 g (4 oz) piece unsmoked
**   bacon**
45 ml (3 tbsp) olive oil
3 garlic cloves
pared rind of ¼ orange
45 ml (3 tbsp) brandy
30 ml (2 tbsp) tomato purée
**   or sun-dried tomato paste**
15 ml (1 tbsp) dried herbes
**   de provence**
600 ml (1 pint) beef stock
salt and pepper
125 g (4 oz) small black olives
chopped parsley, to garnish

PREPARATION TIME
1 hour, plus marinating
COOKING TIME
2-3 hours
FREEZING Suitable

570 CALS PER SERVING

1. To prepare the marinade, pour the wine into a large pan and bring to the boil. Boil vigorously until reduced by half – to 750 ml (1½ pints). Peel and roughly chop the onions, garlic and carrots; chop the celery; bruise the garlic. Add all the marinade ingredients to the wine and stir well. Allow to cool.

2. Trim the meat of any fat or gristle and cut into 6 cm (2½ inch) pieces. Place in a large polythene bag with the marinade. Shake to mix, then seal and leave to marinate in the refrigerator overnight.

3. The next day, pour the contents of the bag into a colander or sieve, set over a bowl to reserve the liquid. Discard vegetables. Pat the meat dry.

4. To prepare the daube, peel and dice the onions; peel and roughly chop the carrots. Cut the bacon into lardons. Heat the oil in a large flameproof casserole, add the bacon lardons and fry until browned. Transfer to a plate, using a slotted spoon. Brown the meat in the fat remaining in the casserole, in batches; transfer to the plate. Brown the onions and carrots in the same way. Return the bacon and meat to the casserole, with the vegetables.

5. Peel and lightly bruise the garlic. Tuck the orange rind and garlic into the daube. Pour over the reserved marinade and brandy. Stir in the tomato purée and herbs. Add enough stock to cover the meat and vegetables. Season well. Bring to a simmer, cover tightly and simmer very gently for 2 hours or until the meat is very tender. (Alternatively cook in the oven at 170°C (325°F) Mark 3 for about 2 hours.) Top up with extra stock if the liquid evaporates too quickly.

6. Stir in the olives and check the seasoning. Let cool completely, then place in the refrigerator overnight. The next day, skim off the fat and discard the orange rind and bay leaves. Reheat before serving, sprinkled with parsley.

VARIATION

If preferred, thicken the cooking liquor with a little beurre manié (see page 36).

TECHNIQUE

Put the meat into a large polythene bag with the wine marinade. Shake to mix, then seal.

SMOKED PORK LOIN WITH SAUPIQUET SAUCE

Thick slices of boiled or baked smoked pork loin are served with a piquant cream and mustard sauce, scented with peppercorns and juniper berries. Serve with a green vegetable, such as cabbage or French beans, and boiled or creamy mashed potatoes.

SERVES 4

700 g (1½ lb) boneless
   smoked pork loin roast
   (see note)
SAUCE
4 shallots
50 g (2 oz) butter
25 g (1 oz) plain flour
300 ml (½ pint) dry white
   wine
300 ml (½ pint) light meat
   or vegetable stock
4 juniper berries, crushed
5 ml (1 tsp) mixed dried
   peppercorns, crushed
50 ml (2 fl oz) white wine
   vinegar
15 ml (1 tbsp) Dijon
   mustard
100 ml (3½ fl oz) crème
   fraîche or double cream
salt and pepper
TO GARNISH
chopped parsley

PREPARATION TIME
20 minutes
COOKING TIME
About 1 hour
FREEZING
Not suitable

530 CALS PER SERVING

1. Boil or bake the pork loin, referring to the package instructions. To boil, place in a saucepan, cover with water and bring to the boil. Lower the heat and simmer for 20 minutes per 450 g (1 lb) plus 20 minutes. Or place in a roasting tin and bake in a preheated oven at 160°C (325°F) Mark 3 for 45 minutes per 450 g (1lb), plus 15 minutes.

2. Meanwhile, peel and chop the shallots. Melt the butter in a saucepan, add the flour and cook, stirring, for about 3 minutes until foaming. Gradually whisk in the wine and stock, then add the juniper berries and half of the shallots. Bring to the boil, stirring, and simmer for 10 minutes.

3. Place the mixed peppercorns, remaining shallots and vinegar in a saucepan and boil to reduce the liquid to 10 ml (2 tsp). Dip the base of the pan into cold water to prevent further reduction. Stir the wine sauce into the reduced vinegar with the mustard. Bring to the boil, lower the heat and simmer for 15-20 minutes until the shallots are cooked. Stir in the cream and bring to the boil. Check the seasoning.

4. To serve, carve the pork loin into thick slices and arrange in a warmed serving dish. Spoon the sauce over the meat and serve at once, garnished with parsley.

NOTE: Pre-packed smoked pork joints are available fron supermarkets. Follow the cooking directions on the package.

The sauce may be strained if preferred, but the peppercorns add colour and texture.

VARIATION

Serve the sauce as an accompaniment to garlicky roast chicken.

TECHNIQUE

When the sauce has simmered for at least 15 minutes and the flavours no longer taste raw, stir in the cream.

TARTE AU ROQUEFORT

Served topped with a tasty garlic and walnut topping, this wonderfully creamy tart is a must for all blue cheese lovers! The sweet crunchy walnuts go perfectly with the strong, salty cheese. A chicory, pear and watercress salad is the ideal complement. If you have time, make the pastry by hand (see page 8).

SERVES 6

PATE BRISEE
250 g (9 oz) plain white flour
5 ml (1 tsp) salt
125 g (4½ oz) butter,
  softened
1 egg yolk (size 1)
ROQUEFORT FILLING
225 g (8 oz) cream cheese,
  at room temperature
150 ml (¼ pint) crème
  fraîche or double cream
3 eggs, beaten
175 g (6 oz) Roquefort
  cheese
pepper
freshly grated nutmeg
45 ml (3 tbsp) chopped fresh
  chives
TOPPING
3 garlic cloves
30 ml (2 tbsp) olive oil
125 g (4 oz) walnut halves
15 ml (1 tbsp) walnut oil
45 ml (3 tbsp) chopped fresh
  parsley

PREPARATION TIME
30 minutes, plus chilling
COOKING TIME
45-50 minutes
FREEZING
Not suitable

905 CALS PER SERVING

1. To make the pastry, sift the flour and salt onto a sheet of greaseproof paper. Put the butter and egg yolk in a food processor and blend until smooth. Shoot in the flour and work until just combined. Turn out onto a lightly floured work surface and knead gently until smooth. Form into a ball, flatten and wrap in cling film. Chill in the refrigerator for at least 30 minutes. Allow to come to room temperature before rolling out.

2. Beat the cream cheese in a bowl until softened, then beat in the cream and eggs. Crumble in the Roquefort and mix gently. Season liberally with pepper and a little nutmeg. As the cheese is salty, you probably won't need to add salt. Stir in the chives; set aside.

3. Preheat the oven to 200°C (400°F) Mark 6. Roll out the pastry on a lightly floured surface and use to line a 25 cm (10 inch) loose-bottomed flan tin. Chill for 20 minutes, then lightly prick the base with a fork. Line the base with greaseproof paper and baking beans and bake blind for 10 minutes. Remove the paper and beans and bake for a further 5 minutes. Let cool slightly. Lower the oven setting to 190°C (375°F) Mark 5.

4. Pour the filling into the pastry case and bake for 30-35 minutes or until puffed and lightly browned.

5. Meanwhile, peel and slice the garlic. Heat the olive oil in a frying pan and add the garlic and walnuts. Stir-fry until the garlic is golden and the walnuts are browned. Stir in the walnut oil and parsley. Serve the tart warm or cold, topped with the warm garlic and walnut topping.

NOTE: Walnuts are cultivated extensively in France. They are at their best freshly harvested, when they are still creamy inside.

TECHNIQUE

Line a 25 cm (10 inch) loose-bottomed fluted flan tin with the pastry, pressing it gently into the edge and flutes.

CREAMY LEEK TART

A delicious creamy flan filled with soft, melting leeks, from Picardy in the north of France. It makes a wonderful picnic dish, but can equally be served warm as a starter, or with a tomato salad as a light lunch. Make the pastry by hand if you have time (see page 8).

SERVES 6

PATE BRISEE
250 g (9 oz) plain white flour
5 ml (1 tsp) salt
125 g (4½ oz) butter,
   softened
1 egg yolk (size 1)
FILLING
1.4 kg (3 lb) leeks, trimmed
50 g (2 oz) butter
salt and pepper
3 egg yolks
300 ml (½ pint) crème
   fraîche or double cream
freshly grated nutmeg

PREPARATION TIME
30 minutes, plus chilling
COOKING TIME
35-40 minutes
FREEZING
Not suitable

640 CALS PER SERVING

1. To make the pastry, sift the flour and salt onto a sheet of greaseproof paper. Put the butter and egg yolk in a food processor and blend until smooth. Shoot in the flour and work until just combined. Turn out onto a lightly floured work surface and knead gently until smooth. Form into a ball, flatten and wrap in cling film. Chill in the refrigerator for at least 30 minutes. Allow to come to room temperature before rolling out.

2. Meanwhile, prepare the filling. Slice or chop the leeks. Melt the butter in a large saucepan, add the leeks and stir to coat in the butter. Add 30 ml (2 tbsp) water, cover and cook gently, stirring occasionally, for about 20 minutes until very soft, but not coloured. Season well. Set aside to cool.

3. Preheat the oven to 200°C (400°F) Mark 6. Roll out the pastry thinly on a lightly floured surface and use to line a 25 cm (10 inch) loose-bottomed flan tin. Chill for 20 minutes, then lightly prick the base with a fork.

4. Beat the egg yolks and cream together, adding a little freshly grated nutmeg. Spread the leeks in the pastry case and pour over the egg and cream mixture.

5. Bake in the oven for 15 minutes, then lower the oven setting to 190°C (375°F) Mark 5 and bake for a further 20-25 minutes until set and browned on top. Serve warm or cold.

VARIATIONS

• Add 125 g (4 oz) chopped Parma ham or *jambon cru du pays* to the filling at stage 4.
• Sprinkle 125 g (4 oz) grated Gruyère over the top of the flan before cooking.
• Make 1½ quantities pastry. Use two thirds to line a pie plate. Chill, add the cooled filling and use the remaining pastry to make a lid. Position, sealing the edges and brushing the top with beaten egg. Make a hole in the centre. Cook as above. Pour a little extra cream into the pie before serving.

TECHNIQUE

Pour the beaten egg and cream mixture evenly over the leek filling.

PISSALADIÈRE

Almost every boulangerie/patisserie in the Midi has their own variation of this famous Provençal onion pizza. Some have a yeast pastry base, others use plain, or even flaky pastry. They may be deep-filled or very thin with a crisp crust, with or without tomatoes on the base. However, you should always find plenty of meltingly soft onions and a generous lattice of olives and anchovies!

SERVES 6

ONION FILLING
1.4 kg (3 lb) mild onions
3 garlic cloves
45 ml (3 tbsp) olive oil
5 ml (1 tsp) dried herbes de provence

YEAST PASTRY
7 g (¼ oz) fresh yeast, 5 ml (1 tsp) fast-action (easy-blend) or 10 ml (2 tsp) ordinary dried yeast
pinch of sugar
150 g (5 oz) plain white flour
50 g (2 oz) butter
1 egg, beaten

TOMATO SAUCE
two 400 g (14 oz) cans chopped tomatoes
45 ml (3 tbsp) tomato purée
30 ml (2 tbsp) olive oil
5 ml (1 tsp) harissa (optional)
150 ml (¼ pint) dry white wine
salt and pepper

TOPPING
about 10 anchovy fillets
extra olive oil, for drizzling
12-18 small black olives

PREPARATION TIME
45 minutes, plus rising
COOKING TIME 2 hours
FREEZING Suitable

475 CALS PER SERVING

1. To make the filling, peel and finely slice the onions and garlic. Heat the oil in a large saucepan, add the onions and garlic and stir well to coat with the oil. Cover tightly and simmer over a very low heat for about 1 hour until meltingly soft, stirring from time to time to prevent them sticking; do not allow them to colour. Add a little water if the onions look dry. Stir in the herbs. Transfer the mixture to a sieve placed over a bowl to drain, reserving the liquid for the yeast dough.

2. To make the yeast dough, cream the fresh yeast in a bowl with the sugar, then whisk in 30 ml (2 tbsp) of the warmed reserved onion liquid. Leave for 10 minutes until frothy. For other yeasts use according to manufacturer's instructions.

3. Sift the flour into a bowl and rub in the butter. Make a well in the centre and add the egg, yeast and a pinch of salt. Mix together with a round-bladed knife, then use your hands to bring the dough together. Knead for 1-2 minutes in the bowl until smooth. Place the bowl and dough inside a large polythene bag and leave to rise for 1 hour or until doubled in size.

4. To make the tomato sauce, place all of the ingredients in a saucepan, mix well and bring to the boil. Simmer, uncovered, for about 1 hour, stirring occasionally, until well reduced and very thick. Season with salt and pepper to taste. Set aside.

5. Preheat the oven to 190°C (375°F) Mark 5. Knock down the dough, knead, then roll out on a lightly floured surface and use to line a shallow rectangular 33 x 20 cm (13 x 8 inch) tin, bringing the dough well up the edges.

6. Spread the reduced tomato sauce thinly over the dough base. Cover with the onions. Halve the anchovy fillets lengthwise and arrange in a lattice on top of the onions. Drizzle with a little olive oil and bake in the oven for about 1 hour until the pastry is golden and crisp. Arrange the olives on top and serve warm or cold.

TECHNIQUE

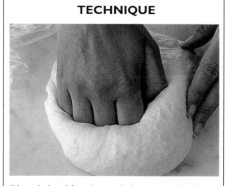

'Knock back' or knead the risen dough for 2-3 minutes to smooth out any large air pockets.

AUBERGINES STUDDED WITH GARLIC AND ROSEMARY

Roasting aubergines in this manner gives them a wonderful aroma and makes them deliciously soft inside. They are equally good served hot or cold, as an accompaniment to grilled or roast meats. Use long, thin aubergines if possible, rather than plump ones.

SERVES 6 - 8

4 medium aubergines
12 fat garlic cloves
handful of fresh rosemary
 sprigs
salt and pepper
olive oil, for basting

PREPARATION TIME
20 minutes
COOKING TIME
45 minutes - 1 hour
FREEZING
Not suitable

110-80 CALS PER SERVING

1. Preheat the oven to 180°C (350°F) Mark 4. Peel the garlic cloves and cut into chunky slivers.

2. Using a small sharp knife, make deep incisions all over each aubergine. Push a sliver of garlic into each one. Insert a small sprig of rosemary into each slit too.

3. Lay the aubergines in a baking dish and drizzle with olive oil. Sprinkle with salt and pepper to taste. Bake in the oven for 45 minutes-1 hour, or until tender.

NOTE: You may prefer to remove the rosemary before serving as it is a little indigestible.

VARIATIONS

• Use courgettes instead of aubergines, but make a line of slits along the top rather than all over.
• Insert lardons of bacon into the slits with the garlic.

TECHNIQUE

Insert a sliver of garlic and a sprig of rosemary into each slit.

ROAST TOMATOES WITH A GARLIC CRUST

In this easy adaptation of the classic stuffed tomato, flavourful cherry or other small tomatoes are baked whole under a delicious crust of chopped garlic, parsley, toasted breadcrumbs and olive oil. It is an excellent accompaniment to chicken and fish dishes.

SERVES 6

6 slices day-old stale bread

6 garlic cloves

45 ml (3 tbsp) chopped fresh parsley

salt and pepper

700 g (1½ lb) cherry or manhattan tomatoes

olive oil, for basting

chopped parsley, to garnish (optional)

PREPARATION TIME
15 minutes
COOKING TIME
15-20 minutes
FREEZING
Not suitable

185 CALS PER SERVING

1. Preheat the oven to 220°C (425°F) Mark 7. Tear up the bread and place in a food processor or blender. Process until you have fine breadcrumbs; there should be approximately 125 g (4 oz). Place in a heavy-based frying pan and dry-fry over a moderate heat until golden.

2. Peel and finely chop the garlic. Stir into the breadcrumbs with the chopped parsley and salt and pepper to taste.

3. Place the tomatoes in a shallow roasting tin or dish, positioning them close together and in a single layer. Sprinkle the breadcrumbs evenly over the tomatoes and drizzle liberally with olive oil.

4. Bake in the oven for 15-20 minutes until the crust is golden and the tomatoes are soft. The tomatoes will have disintegrated slightly under the crust. Scatter with more parsley to serve if you like.

VARIATIONS

• Instead of cherry tomatoes, use halved plum tomatoes. Place in the dish, cut-side up, then apply the topping.
• Add 50 g (2 oz) chopped anchovies to the crust.

TECHNIQUE

Drizzle the olive oil evenly and liberally over the breadcrumb topping.

GARLIC POTATO CAKE

Thin potato sticks are tossed with garlic and thyme and cooked in a frying pan to a golden, crisp cake – rather like a robust rösti. It is a good accompaniment to serve with roast meats and chicken dishes.

SERVES 6

700 g (1½ lb) potatoes
6 garlic cloves, crushed
30 ml (2 tbsp) chopped
   fresh thyme
salt and pepper
125 g (4 oz) unsalted butter

PREPARATION TIME
20 minutes
COOKING TIME
35-40 minutes
FREEZING
Not suitable

240 CALS PER SERVING

1. Preheat the oven to 200°C (400 °F) Mark 6. Peel the potatoes and immerse in a bowl of cold water. Drain the potatoes, slice thinly, then cut into thin sticks, a little thicker than matchsticks. Place in a bowl and don't worry if they brown a little – this won't be apparent once cooked.

2. Add the garlic and thyme to the potato matchsticks and toss well. Season liberally with salt and pepper.

3. To clarify the butter, slowly melt the butter in a small pan, then skim off any impurities. Keep warm.

4. Pour 30 ml (2 tbsp) of the butter into a heavy-based 25 cm (10 inch) non-stick frying pan, suitable for use in the oven (see note). Transfer the potato sticks to the pan, spread evenly and press down firmly to form a 'cake'. Pour over the remaining butter.

5. Place the pan over a moderate heat and cook for 5 minutes or until the underside begins to turn golden brown. To check, carefully lift up the edge of the potato cake with a palette knife.

6. Press the potatoes down firmly once more and cover with a lid or a buttered sheet of foil. Bake in the oven for 25-30 minutes, or until the potatoes are tender when pierced with a sharp knife and the underside is a deep golden brown.

7. Place a lid or plate on top of the potato cake, invert onto the lid and slide back into the pan. Cook over a medium heat for 5 minutes, or until golden and crisp. Loosen the cake with a palette knife so that it moves freely.

8. Place a warmed serving plate over the pan and invert the potato cake onto the plate. Serve immediately.

NOTE: The Le Creuset range includes a non-stick skillet with an integral metal handle which can be placed in the oven.

VARIATION

Sauté 125 g (4 oz) diced bacon or lardons in a non-stick pan until golden, then stir into the raw potato. Cook as above and serve as a light lunch or supper, with a tomato salad.

TECHNIQUE

To prepare the clarified butter, slowly melt the unsalted butter in a small pan over a low heat, then skim off the white residue or foam from the surface.

TARTE AU FROMAGE FRAIS

This deliciously rich, creamy baked cheesecake enclosed in a crisp, sweet pastry case is covered with glistening ripe fresh figs and lightly grilled to brown. If preferred, top with strawberries rather than figs. Make the pastry by hand if you have time (see page 9).

SERVES 6

PATE SUCREE

175 g (6 oz) plain white flour

2.5 ml (½ tsp) salt

75 g (3 oz) butter, softened

75 g (3 oz) sugar

3 egg yolks

2.5 ml (½ tsp) vanilla
essence

FILLING

225 g (8 oz) fromage frais
(not low-fat)

50 g (2 oz) butter, softened

110 g (4 oz) caster sugar or
vanilla sugar

2 eggs, beaten

8 ripe black figs

30 ml (2 tbsp) redcurrant
jelly

PREPARATION TIME
35 minutes, plus chilling
COOKING TIME
40-45 minutes
FREEZING
Not suitable

540 CALS PER SERVING

1. To make the pastry, sift the flour and salt onto a sheet of greaseproof paper. Place the butter, sugar, egg yolks and vanilla essence in a food processor and blend until smooth. Shoot in the flour and blend until just combined. Turn onto a lightly floured surface and knead gently until smooth. Form into a ball, flatten and wrap in cling film. Chill in the refrigerator for at least 30 minutes.

2. Preheat the oven to 190°C (375°F) Mark 5. To make the filling, beat the fromage frais, butter and sugar together in a bowl. Gradually beat in the eggs, then set aside.

3. Roll out the pastry thinly on a lightly floured surface and use to line a 23 cm (9 inch) flan tin. Prick the base and line with greaseproof paper and baking beans. Bake blind for 10 minutes, then remove the paper and beans and bake for a further 5 minutes until just coloured.

4. Pour the filling into the pastry case and bake in the oven for 25-30 minutes until risen and brown. Leave to cool in the tin for 10 minutes, then transfer to a wire rack and allow to cool completely.

5. Preheat the grill to high. Halve or quarter the figs and arrange on top of the tart. Warm the redcurrant jelly and lightly brush over the figs. Place the tart under the grill, close to the element, until the figs are lightly browned. Serve immediately.

NOTE: To prevent over-browning, protect the pastry edge with a rim of foil during grilling.

VARIATION

For the topping, replace the figs with 175 g (6 oz) sliced strawberries. Glaze as above.

TECHNIQUE

Use the pastry to line a 23 cm (9 inch) fluted flan tin, gently pressing the pastry into the flutes and edge of the tin.

GOLDEN CUSTARD TART

Versions of this golden custard tart – known as *flan* – are found in pâtisseries throughout France. Here the vanilla-scented custard is encased in a buttery brioche yeast pastry with a pretty lattice top. A tart compote of plums is the perfect complement.

SERVES 6

BRIOCHE PASTRY

10 ml (2 tsp) ordinary dried
   or 5 ml (1 tsp) easy-blend
   (fast-action) dried yeast
60 ml (4 tbsp) milk
25 g (1 oz) caster sugar
350 g (12 oz) strong plain
   white flour
5 ml (1 tsp) salt
3 eggs, at room
   temperature, beaten
125 g (4 oz) unsalted butter,
   softened

PLUM COMPOTE

450 g (1 lb) plums
50 g (2 oz) caster sugar
strip of lemon rind
1 cinnamon stick
2 cloves

FLAN CUSTARD

150 ml (¼ pint) milk
150 ml (¼ pint) cream
1 vanilla pod, split
3 eggs
125 g (4 oz) caster or vanilla
   sugar
45 ml (3 tbsp) plain flour

PREPARATION TIME
30 minutes, plus rising
COOKING TIME
1 hour
FREEZING
Not suitable

640 CALS PER SERVING

1. If using ordinary dried yeast, place in a bowl with the warmed 60 ml (4 tbsp) milk and a pinch of the sugar. Cover and leave in a warm place for 10 minutes until frothy.

2. Sift the flour and salt into a bowl. Add the remaining sugar and easy-blend yeast, if using. Make a well in the centre. Add the eggs and yeast mixture or 60 ml (4 tbsp) milk.

3. Mix to a soft elastic dough, adding a little more flour if necessary, but keeping the dough quite soft. Work in the softened butter until smooth, shiny and elastic. Cover and leave to rise in a warm place for 2-4 hours until doubled in size. Knock back, then wrap and chill for about 30 minutes until firm enough to roll out.

4. Meanwhile, halve and stone the plums. Place in a saucepan with the sugar and 300 ml (½ pint) water. Bring to the boil, then simmer for 10-20 minutes until just tender. Remove with a slotted spoon. Add the lemon rind and spices to the liquid and boil until reduced and syrupy. Strain over the plums, let cool, then chill.

5. To make the custard, heat the milk and cream together with the vanilla pod until almost boiling. Set aside to infuse for 15 minutes, then strain. Beat the eggs and sugar together until pale and creamy. Beat in the flour, then the warm milk and cream.

6. Cut off one third of the pastry, re-wrap and chill. Roll out the other two thirds and use to line a 26 x 19 cm (10¾ x 7½ inch) base-measurement rectangular fluted loose-bottomed tart tin. Pour in the custard and leave in a warm place to rise for 20 minutes.

7. Preheat the oven to 200°C (400°F) Mark 6. Bake tart for 15-20 minutes or until the custard starts to set. Lower oven setting to 170°C (325°F) Mark 3.

8. Roll out remaining pastry and cut into strips. Arrange in a lattice over the flan; brush pastry with beaten egg (see technique). Bake for 45 minutes until golden and set. Cool in tin. Serve at room temperature, with the plums.

TECHNIQUE

Arrange the pastry strips over the partially cooked flan, using beaten egg to stick the strips to the sides.

PEAR TARTE RENVERSÉE

This mouth-watering upside down pear tart is cooked in a similar way to a tarte tatin. Halved pears are poached in a red wine syrup on the hob in an ovenproof pan, then covered with pastry and baked. Inverted to serve, the tart is equally delicious hot, warm or cold, with crème fraîche.

SERVES 6

PATE BRISEE
225 g (8 oz) plain white flour
5 ml (1 tsp) salt
110 g (4 oz) butter, softened
30 ml (2 tbsp) sugar
1 egg yolk, size 1
PEAR FILLING
8 medium under-ripe pears
1 cinnamon stick
75 g (3 oz) caster sugar
600 ml (1 pint) full-bodied
 red wine
TO DECORATE
toasted slivered almonds

PREPARATION TIME
45 minutes
COOKING TIME
1 hour 40 minutes
FREEZING
Not suitable

495 CALS PER SERVING

1. To make the pastry, sift the flour and salt onto a sheet of greaseproof paper. Place the butter, sugar and egg yolk in a food processor and blend until smooth. Shoot in the flour and process until just combined. Turn out onto a lightly floured surface and knead gently until smooth. Form into a ball, flatten and wrap in cling film. Chill in the refrigerator for at least 30 minutes. Allow to come to room temperature before rolling out.

2. Meanwhile, peel the pears, halve lengthwise and carefully scoop out the core, with a teaspoon or melon-baller. Arrange the pear halves in a circular fashion in a 25 cm (10 inch) heavy-based non-stick metal dish or frying pan (suitable for use in the oven), positioning them with the tapering stalk ends towards the centre. Use the remaining pears to fill any spaces.

3. Crumble the cinnamon over the top and sprinkle over the sugar. Pour on the red wine and bring to the boil. Cover and simmer gently for about 1 hour or until tender.

4. Preheat the oven to 200°C (400°F) Mark 6. Uncover the pan and position a plate over the pears to hold them in place while you drain off the juices into a saucepan. Boil the juices hard until reduced and very syrupy, then drizzle over the pears.

5. Roll out the pastry to a round, slightly larger than the diameter of the pan. Lift the pastry over the pears, roll in the edges and press down inside the rim. Bake in the oven for about 35-40 minutes until the pastry is crisp and golden.

6. To serve hot, invert the tart onto a plate, taking care to avoid the hot juices burning your fingers. If serving cold, allow to cool and invert the tart only when ready to serve, otherwise the juices will make the pastry soggy. Sprinkle with toasted almonds and serve with crème fraîche.

VARIATION

Use apples instead of pears and ground cloves rather than cinnamon.

TECHNIQUE

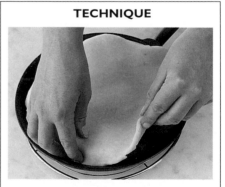

Roll in the edges of the pastry, then press down the side of the tin to form a pastry rim around the pears.

TARTELETTES AU CITRON

These light souffléd lemon tartlets are cooked until just setting, dusted with icing sugar and cooked again until lightly browned. If you have time, make the pastry by hand (see page 8). Serve the tartlettes with the crème fraîche and fresh raspberries.

SERVES 8

PATE BRISEE
200 g (7 oz) plain white flour
2.5 ml (¹/₂ tsp) salt
100 g (3¹/₂ oz) butter,
   softened
45 ml (3 tbsp) sugar
I egg yolk
LEMON FILLING
4 eggs, separated
150 g (5 oz) caster sugar
finely grated rind of 2
   lemons
juice of I lemon
pinch of salt
TO FINISH
icing sugar, for dusting
raspberries, to decorate

PREPARATION TIME
35 minutes, plus chilling
COOKING TIME
20 minutes
FREEZING
Not suitable

325 CALS PER SERVING

I. To make the pastry, sift the flour and salt onto a sheet of greaseproof paper. Place the butter, sugar and egg yolk in a food processor and blend until smooth. Shoot in the flour and blend until just combined. Turn out onto a lightly floured surface and knead gently until smooth. Form into a ball, flatten and wrap in cling film. Chill for at least 30 minutes. Bring to room temperature before rolling out.

2. Preheat the oven to 180°C (350°F) Mark 4. Roll out the pastry and use to line 8 individual 10 cm (4 inch) loose-bottomed flan tins. Prick the bases with a fork and line with greaseproof paper and baking beans. Bake blind for 10 minutes, then remove paper and beans and return to the oven for 5 minutes until set and beginning to brown. Allow to cool. Lower the oven setting to 170°C (325°F) Mark 3.

3. To make the filling, whisk the egg yolks and 75 g (3 oz) sugar together in a bowl until pale, mousse-like, and thick enough to leave a trail (see technique). Whisk in the lemon rind and juice. Set the bowl over a pan of simmering water and stir until the mixture thickens enough to coat the back of a wooden spoon. Allow to cool.

4. Whisk the egg whites with the salt until stiff but not dry. Gradually whisk in the remaining sugar, a spoonful at a time. Beat a spoonful of the meringue into the lemon custard to loosen it, then carefully fold in the remainder.

5. Spoon filling into the tartlet cases, set on a baking sheet and bake for 15-20 minutes until beginning to rise. Sprinkle with icing sugar and return to the oven for 4-5 minutes until just beginning to brown. Serve warm, hot or cold, with crème fraîche and raspberries.

NOTE: The filling rises on baking, but will sink again as it cools.

VARIATIONS

Use 2 small oranges or 3 limes instead of the lemons.

TECHNIQUE

For the filling, whisk the egg yolks with 75 g (3 oz) sugar until the mixture is pale, mousse-like and thick enough to leave a ribbon trail when the beaters are lifted.

CHOCOLATE CRÈME BRÛLÉE

This classic crème brûleé, topped with its melted crust of demerara sugar, is made extra rich with the darkest chocolate. It is important to cook the custard until properly thickened so that it will set in the pots or ramekins, however it must not boil or all will be lost and curdled! Prepare the crèmes the day before you intend to serve them.

SERVES 6-8

450 ml (¾ pint) double
 cream
60 ml (4 tbsp) milk
1 vanilla pod, split
6 egg yolks
50 g (2 oz) caster sugar
75 g (3 oz) bitter chocolate
demerara sugar, for
 sprinkling

PREPARATION TIME
15 minutes, plus infusing
COOKING TIME
20 minutes, plus overnight
chilling
FREEZING
Not suitable

500-380 CALS PER SERVING

1. Pour the cream and milk into a saucepan. Scrape the vanilla seeds into the cream, adding the pod as well. Bring slowly to the boil, then turn off the heat and leave to infuse for 15 minutes.

2. Whisk the egg yolks and sugar together in a bowl until pale and creamy. Place the chocolate in a food processor or blender and process to break it up. Remove the vanilla pod from the cream.

3. With the motor running, pour the hot cream into the food processor and whizz until the chocolate is melted and the mixture is smooth. Pour this over the whisked egg and sugar mixture and stir well. Return to the saucepan and stir with a wooden spoon over a low heat for about 20 minutes until thickened; don't allow to boil or it will curdle.

4. Strain the mixture into a jug, then pour into the ramekins, filling them to the top; the custard will sink as it cools. Do not cover, but cool completely. Chill overnight to set.

5. Preheat the grill to its hottest setting. Sprinkle a very thin even layer of sugar over the surface of each custard; it should be about 1 sugar grain thick. Set the ramekins on a sturdy baking tray and place under the grill as close to the element as possible. Watch carefully and remove as soon as the sugar caramelises. Leave to cool completely, then chill again before serving.

NOTE: As an alternative to grilling, you can wave a blow-torch over the custards to melt the sugar. Practice this first, taking all safety precautions!

VARIATION

Add 15 ml (1 tbsp) quality instant coffee to the cream for a mocha flavour.

TECHNIQUE

With the food processor motor running, pour in the hot cream through the feeder tube and whizz until the chocolate is melted.

WALNUT CAKE WITH CRÈME ANGLAISE

Walnuts are grown extensively throughout France and each region has its culinary specialities. They lend a superb flavour and texture to this moist rich nut cake, which is served on a pool of delicate brandy-flavoured custard and drizzled with caramel sauce.

SERVES 6-8

WALNUT CAKE

150 g (5 oz) unsalted butter, softened

125 g (4 oz) caster sugar

4 eggs, separated

finely grated rind of 1 lemon

90 ml (6 tbsp) fine dry brown breadcrumbs

150 g (5 oz) walnuts

CREME ANGLAISE

300 ml (½ pint) milk

1 vanilla pod, split

15 ml (1 tbsp) caster sugar

2 egg yolks, beaten

30 ml (2 tbsp) cognac or armagnac

CARAMEL SYRUP

125 g (4 oz) caster sugar

TO DECORATE

8-12 walnut halves

PREPARATION TIME
45 minutes
COOKING TIME
1 hour
FREEZING
Suitable

705 - 530 CALS PER SERVING

1. Preheat the oven to 170°C (325°F) Mark 3. Brush a 23 cm (9 inch) spring-form cake tin with melted butter, allow to set, then dust out with flour. Line the base with non-stick baking parchment.

2. In a bowl, cream the butter with 75 g (3 oz) sugar until pale and creamy. Beat in the egg yolks, one at a time, then the lemon rind and breadcrumbs.

3. Finely grind the walnuts in a blender or food processor; do not over-process or they will become oily. Fold into the egg mixture.

4. In another bowl, whisk the egg whites until stiff but not dry. Whisk in the remaining sugar, until stiff and shiny. Gently fold into the cake mixture. Spoon into the cake tin, level the surface and bake for about 1 hour until risen and firm to the touch. To test, insert a skewer into the middle — it should come out clean. Remove from tin and cool on a wire rack.

5. To make the crème anglaise, put the milk, sugar and vanilla pod in a saucepan and bring almost to the boil. Set aside to infuse for 15 minutes. Remove vanilla pod. Pour onto the egg yolks, whisking. Return to the pan and stir over a low heat until thickened enough to coat the back of the wooden spoon. Pour into a cold bowl and stir in the cognac. Cover, cool, then chill.

6. For the caramel sauce, put the sugar in a small heavy-based saucepan with 30 ml (2 tbsp) water. Heat gently to dissolve, then boil steadily to a deep golden brown caramel. Remove from heat and carefully add 90 ml (6 tbsp) cold water; it will splutter and harden. Stir over a low heat until melted, then boil until syrupy. Dip the walnuts into the caramel, turning to coat them.

7. Pool a little custard on each serving plate and place a thin slice of cake on top. Decorate with the walnuts and drizzle with caramel to serve.

TECHNIQUE

Using a large metal spoon, gently fold the meringue into the cake mixture.

PÈCHES CARDINAL

For this classic dessert poached peaches are served on a bed of vanilla ice cream, cloaked in a fresh raspberry sauce. Escoffier created this dish and named it *cardinal* because of the crimson colour of the sauce. You may prefer to omit the poaching, serving the peaches fresh with the ice cream and sauce.

SERVES 6

VANILLA ICE CREAM
2 vanilla pods
300 ml (½ pint) milk
300 ml (½ pint) double
  cream
6 egg yolks
110 g (4 oz) caster sugar
POACHED PEACHES
125 g (4 oz) caster sugar
1 vanilla pod, split
6 ripe peaches
RASPBERRY SAUCE
225 g (8 oz) raspberries
15 ml (1 tbsp) kirsch
caster sugar, to taste
TO FINISH
125 g (4 oz) almonds
  (optional)

PREPARATION TIME
1 hour
COOKING TIME
25 minutes, plus freezing
FREEZING
Suitable: Ice cream only

655 CALS PER SERVING

1. To make the ice cream, split the vanilla pods and place in a saucepan with the milk and cream. Bring almost to the boil, then remove from the heat and leave to infuse for 15 minutes. Remove the vanilla pod.

2. Beat the egg yolks and sugar together in a bowl, then pour on the hot milk, stirring well. Return to the pan and stir over a gentle heat with a wooden spoon until the custard thickens enough to coat the back of the spoon. Strain into a cold bowl, cover, cool and chill thoroughly.

3. Churn in an ice-cream maker according to the manufacturer's instructions until frozen, then transfer to a freezerproof container and place in the freezer (see note). If you do not have an ice-cream maker, freeze the ice cream in a shallow container, whisking periodically during freezing to break down the ice crystals.

4. For the peaches, place the sugar and split vanilla pod in a saucepan with 300 ml (½ pint) water and bring slowly to the boil. Skim and cool. Meanwhile, skin the peaches (see technique), then carefully halve and remove the stones. Bring the sugar syrup to a simmer. Add the peach halves and poach at a bare simmer for 15 minutes or until tender. Cool completely, then discard the vanilla pod.

5. For the sauce, place the raspberries in a saucepan and heat gently until the juices just start to run. Purée in a blender or food processor, then sieve to remove the pips. Stir in the kirsch and sugar to taste.

6. Skin the almonds if using by briefly immersing in boiling water, then slipping off the skins. Halve lengthwise and shred finely.

7. Scoop the vanilla ice cream into a glass serving dish. Arrange the peach halves on top and drizzle over the raspberry sauce. Sprinkle with the slivered almonds, if using, and serve immediately.

NOTE: Transfer the ice cream to the refrigerator for at least 30 minutes before serving to soften.

TECHNIQUE

To skin peaches, briefly immerse in boiling water, remove and slip off the skins.

GREEN APPLE SORBET WITH MADELEINES

Serve this fresh, summery sorbet with a pile of lemony madeleines on a balmy evening. Select sweet, but sharp, Granny Smith apples – taste one first! The madeleines are best served while still warm.

SERVES 4

SORBET

450 g (1 lb) Granny Smith
  apples
about 50 g (2 oz) caster
  sugar
30 ml (2 tbsp) lemon or lime
  juice
45 ml (3 tbsp) Calvados
few drops of green food
  colouring (optional)
1 egg white (optional)

MADELEINES

125 g (4 oz) plain white flour
5 ml (1 tsp) baking powder
4 eggs
125 g (4 oz) caster sugar
finely grated rind of 1 lemon
  or lime
125 g (4 oz) unsalted butter,
  melted

TO SERVE

icing sugar, for dusting
60 ml (4 tbsp) Calvados
finely pared apple peel, to
  decorate (optional)

PREPARATION TIME
25 minutes, plus chilling and
freezing
COOKING TIME
10 minutes
FREEZING Suitable

130 CALS PER SERVING

1. To make the sorbet, peel, halve and core the apples. Place in a saucepan with the sugar and lemon or lime juice. Cover and simmer for 5-10 minutes until tender. Purée in a blender or food processor, then sieve to remove any lumps. Cool, chill, then stir in the Calvados and colouring, if using. Churn in an ice-cream maker according to the manufacturer's instructions, adding the lightly beaten egg white if using, halfway through freezing (see note).

2. For the madeleines, sift the flour and baking powder together. Whisk the eggs, sugar and lemon or lime rind together in a bowl until thick and mousse-like. Carefully fold in half the flour. Pour in half of the warm (not hot) butter around the edge of the bowl and carefully fold in. Repeat with the remaining flour and butter, then chill in the refrigerator for at least 45 minutes, until considerably thickened.

3. Preheat the oven to 230°C (450°F) Mark 8. Brush two 12-hole madeleine tins with melted butter. Allow to set, then dust out with flour. Two-thirds fill each mould with the mixture. Bake for 5 minutes, then lower the setting to 200°C (400°F) Mark 6 and bake for a further 5 minutes or until risen and firm. Turn out onto a wire rack.

4. To serve, pile the madeleines onto a serving plate and dust with icing sugar. Scoop the sorbet into chilled serving dishes and drizzle a little Calvados over each portion. Decorate with twists of apple peel if desired. Serve at once, with the madeleines.

NOTE: If you do not have an ice-cream maker, freeze in a shallow container, whisking periodically to break down the ice crystals. When the sorbet is almost frozen, break up with a fork, stir in the whisked egg white and freeze.

Resting the madeleine batter before baking gives the cakes their characteristic dense texture. The above quantity makes 24; each provides 85 calories.

TECHNIQUE

Pour half of the lukewarm butter around the edge of the mixture, then carefully fold in, using a large metal spoon.

If you would like further information about the **Good Housekeeping Cookery Club**, please write to:
Penny Smith, Ebury Press, Random House, 20 Vauxhall Bridge Road, London SW1V 2SA.